CW00673316

A GAME OF
THROWS

CELEBRATING 50 YEARS OF JUDO

A GAME OF THROWS

CELEBRATING 50 YEARS OF JUDO

Neil Adams MBE

FOXGLOVES

foxglovesmartialarts.com
foxspirit.co.uk

conversion by T.J. Everley

Edited by Alasdair Stuart

Image credits at rear

ISBN: 978-1-909348-96-7

First Edition

This is an autobiographical work and as such while every effort has
been made to verify details given, events, locales and conversations have
been recreated from memory and it is those recollections that are presented
herein.

Published by:
Fox Spirit Books
www.foxspirit.co.uk
adele@foxspirit.co.uk

adele@foxspirit.co.uk

Contents

Foreword

by John Goodbody

Neil Adams stands on the highest plinth in the pantheon of British male judo fighters. It is not just his unmatched record in competitions, which includes two Olympic finals, becoming the first British man to win a world title as well as five European senior titles that justifies that statement. It was his range of technical expertise that is so memorable. Watch the you-tube film of the light-middleweight final in Maastricht in 1981 and you will see a variety of moves that few competitors and no Briton has ever matched. I was fortunate enough to be present that day and never tire of watching that demolition of Jiri Kase time and again.

In my 50 years of reporting the sport, I have not seen any Japanese so outclassed among the lighter weight categories by any foreigner. Many people, whose opinion has profound substance, have told me of the expertise of John Newman but I never saw him fight before he retired. However, I can confidently say that Neil has been supreme in the last half century of international competition.

Neil's upright stance, ability to throw both sides, skilful transition into newaza, especially into his famous ju-ji-gatame meant that he was admired across the world. And his amenable personality meant that he was much liked as well. The Japanese called him 'Happo Bigin' (everyone's friend).

It was natural that because of his ability to demonstrate and analyse his own range of skills, he would move into coaching after retiring. Many people have benefitted from his advice and tutelage. His fluency and understanding of judo have also meant that he has a proved a widely admired television commentator, satisfying both people involved in the sport and also interesting the large numbers of uninformed viewers. Neil's continuing contribution to judo remains immense.

JOHN GOODBODY covered the 2016 Olympics for The Sunday Times, his 13th successive Summer Games and is the author of the audio book A History of the Olympics, read by Barry Davies, the BBC commentator. He was Sports News Correspondent of The Times 1986-2007, for whom he received journalistic awards in all three decades on the paper, including Sports Reporter of The Year in 2001.

4 decades of Neil Adams: 80's, 90's, 00's 10's

1. Introduction

33 years ago, almost to the day; I did an autobiography with Nicolas Soames, who wrote it for me. I said that I wasn't altogether happy with the way it was written and I didn't mean the way he wrote it but the way I came across in the book. I wasn't happy with the 23 year old that was evident in the book. Now that I look back, after all these years, I can see that I was a different person and not only that, it only covered part of my life; the competition part of my life and my early relationships.

But was that the real me?

What about the man I am as well as the man I was?

A lot's happened in the intervening years, the vast majority of it good. So what we decided to do is to go back 35 years and do a reflection of everything that is in this book and have a look at this 23 year old and the last book and how it depicts me as a person and just to see how I've changed.

There are parts of that book, *A Life in Judo* that really do grate on me and I think it's because of how I come across really. I'm all for confidence and I think that I've always been confident but I think that there's a kind of arrogance that comes with that confidence that comes across. I didn't really care as much as I should have at that time of my life.

It wasn't so much that I don't like who I was back then, more like people didn't really have a chance to really know ME. When you're that young and that high up a profession, it all becomes a persona. I think I maybe hid behind that, believed the hype a little too much. And that's not healthy. It makes for a bigger fall when it's all over or doesn't go right.

If I could chat to my 23 year old self, one of the things I would tell him, is that you've got to make sure that you get your preparation right and that you show respect. Whether you're a winner or a loser you have to show respect and to be nice. It's not that I wasn't nice, in my heart I've never changed. I've always been a nice person, I think, and people have always liked me, but I had a time in my life when people were a little bit wary of the grit and determination of the athlete that wanted to achieve so much. So I think; I would have liked to have been a little bit softer in the approach and also to think more about the things I rushed into, things that affected my personality, affected my direction.

Yes, I think that relationships definitely affected certain parts of my competition life, and I think my competition life sometimes affected my relationships. I also think that I'm in a much better place now. I'm very settled in my mind and in my heart. I have my beautiful family, who are the number one priority in my life. So if I looked at anything over the last 30 years, the thing that has changed dramatically is that my absolute Number One priority as a 23 year old, was to be best in the world, and now my Number One priority is to be the best dad and best husband in the world. So I guess we do change priorities. They change as we get older and we look at things a little bit differently.

That's where this book comes in. Here, we're going to talk about not just the mountain I was scaling when I was 23, but what happened when I got to the top of it, what happened when I realised I had to come down, and how my life has changed. It's been a long, gruelling fight but it's made me who I am.

And that's just it.

To the core, I am a fighter and always will be. You'll soon see that at times I was a victim of circumstance. Although; some of the decisions I made, both consciously and unconsciously, educated or through naivety, were not the best, that at times painted me into a dark corner.

This book is to show how I never let the dark consume me completely, that the fighter was always there waiting for its time, the permission to come forth, and although I had help from other at times to clear the fog, it always had to come from me. The permission to live and leave a legacy could only come from one person. These are the events that have led me here.

So, let's go meet me.

Cyril coaching Neil and Chris

2. Beginning

I started early. I remember doing the Midland area championships at 7 or 8 years old and my dad said he'd put me in for a competition. I didn't know the rules or how to play the game really, but I remember being in the competition and fighting my heart out. I remember being held down and fighting my way out and my dad said 'you're not listening to me, you're just not listening'. I won but it was a close fight.

The thing is, the fact I almost lost didn't bother him. What bothered him really, was that I hadn't listened.

I remember my dad berating me, and thinking 'well I'm not going to let that happen again'. I got this medal, and one of the top coaches came up and said 'that was amazing, your kid's going to do well'. That was my first Judo medal and first step into competition.

It was pretty stretched out back then, there weren't competitions every weekend. It was tough keeping momentum, especially when you were so young. I remember doing my first nationals. I lost and after the fight my dad said 'if you want to do this you'll need to apply yourself more'. I won the next five, and then I won the Under 18s, then Under 21s, and the seniors, and it went on and on. You get the picture. I always learned from my losses. That's the most important thing, I find, and something I teach now. If there is a life lesson to be learned through sport, it's that: take everything as a lesson, a win or a loss, and get back into it.

Funnily enough, I found myself doing the same as my dad did just a few years ago. I was watching my daughter fight and yelled across the mat that she wasn't listening. That she needed to look at me to get directions. Exact same altercation. Exact same tone of voice. Judo never changes. Or maybe it's a case of Judo Dads never change?

I started young and Dad worked us hard but I now see that he was very clever about it. He never entered Chris, my brother, and I into every competition. He tried to give us a wide physical education and keep our minds open to new sports. That was if we found something we liked, great, and even if we didn't, everything we did was inter-related. For example, gymnastics and trampolining in particular are all about all-over body strength, muscle control and flexibility. So is Judo. It's all about capability.

We've done the same with our two girls and I tried with Ashley too. The most important thing with them, like Dad did with us, is this;

You don't have to do it. You *NEVER* have to do it.

I see so many parents pushing their kids into sports and it breaks my heart. Nothing will make a child who isn't physically confident miserable faster than pushing them into something that frightens them. And nothing will give that kid the confidence they need faster than letting them learn what they enjoy and study at their own pace.

Of course, it is different from one personality to the next. I found that out when I met Jimmy Pedro. Jimmy was a great competitor from America: World Champ, 2 x Olympic medallist and he came to train with me when he was very young at my training school in Coventry. His father pushed him. He pushed him hard. But Jimmy also has great admiration for his father, and he always says 'if he hadn't pushed me I wouldn't have achieved what I did'.

It's all about mind set and knowing what buttons to press. My dad didn't need to push me and I think that probably he recognised that. He also realised it was much better if it came from me. Everybody is individual; Jimmy Pedro's dad probably realised if he didn't do it, Jimmy would maybe have been stuck in front of the television or the equivalent. Jimmy can now say he is World Champion and with whomever, and however he got there, I know he is thankful.

So I think you have to understand the person, athlete and individual. Judo is an individual sport. Great coaches know how the student ticks and then how to tweak it because that's the important aspect of it. My dad certainly knew how to tweak me and get me flowing the right direction. The fine tuning, though came later and that came from some hard lessons learned.

***

So I competed quite happily at junior levels and then aged 16 I went to London. London was always the mecca. I had to go there to train as that's where you went if you wanted to train with the best people in the world, or at least the best the UK had on offer at the time. I'd arranged to live in a house with several Judo people. I had my own kind of apartment. My mother was 39 years old at the time and was quiet all the way down. My dad was trying to make light of it all: 'you'll be fine', he would chirp, you're going to do this, you're going to do that. My mother didn't say a thing. It's something I've experienced since, as a dad, when I've dropped my son off at university and it felt as if my heart was being ripped out. My mother must have felt that and I remember the tears on her face, the absolute pain of letting her son, her youngest son, her 16 year old, go. I was on the doorstep, it came the time for them to leave. We were putting it off and putting it off… I think you could actually hear the apron strings rip as they got in the car and drove away. It was a strange moment, as I was stinging with melancholy to be leaving that 'boyhood' life behind, but as well, for me, it was going to be a bit of an adventure.

I didn't really realise until I was on my own in the room and then I thought, 'oh my God'.

I can still see her going off into the distance with tears streaming down her face. It was only 100 miles from her, not that far, but in those days I had no transport or money for train fares, so it could have been 1,000 miles.

The first thing I did was to go into my room and I lay down on the bed. I'd never been alone before. It was difficult to cope with that, however, I knew that on the following Monday I had a job interview in Shepherd's Bush, so that was a big push in the right direction, really. As I waiting for that, I introduced myself to people in the house. I was just a kid, a young boy, really, but a young boy with a purpose, an ambition and determination and I would have done anything to survive. There were times, hard times... we talk about stealing milk off milk floats? I guess it is stealing. I saw it as borrowing, and I've still yet to pay them back but, truly, I was borrowing.

It got to the stage where I didn't have money... I should have got a bike, a bike would have cost me 40 or 50 quid at the time and I could have just cycled everywhere, but for some strange reason I didn't. I ran everywhere, which in some ways was a good thing for me because I was in good condition. More importantly from a mental perspective it taught me to focus, to be alone, and that was, is actually, still one of the hardest things for me, to be alone.

This is how rough things were then: At one point, I was living in Peckham, I needed a gym and a sauna so I went into this local gym. I didn't know it was owned by the Krays. I told the guy at the front desk who I was and that 'I was going to be the next World Champion, adding that 'you need to invest in me'! This guy threw his head back and started laughing at me. He smiled and said, 'I'd better help you then'. I said 'thank you' and he gave me a membership. Easy as that. Saying that, I used to go there sometimes in the sauna and some of the conversations I used to hear were a little bit dodgy to say the least but they were always behind me, always asking 'how did the competition go?'

Wonderful stories and great times. The funny thing about those types of people, they're very loyal, very loyal to their own. And fortunately for me, they decided I was one of them.

But it was so hard. Hardly any money, running everywhere, constantly fighting for respect. It wasn't even that I was unsupported. I was getting money from The Sports Aid Foundation, but it wasn't enough to live. My parents were fantastic, they helped wherever they could. But they didn't have a lot of money, it's not like they could give me £200 a month to help me live, so I was really having to work my passage. My full time training was having to run to work, run back from work, do my weight training and full time Judo in the evening. I wasn't really training full time until they decided I had real potential, then they gave me a proper Sports Aid Foundation grant. It was when I first won the European Championships I started getting endorsements.

I was the first to get endorsements of any Judoka in the UK, from a vitamin company, then I got a car given to me by a rental car company – Budget Rental Car. That was great for me then. I had made it! I was rich! I had a really good life and money. Top athletes now, they have the same situation, they get prize money to help them go from one event to another, but there are more athletes that are struggling. It's a catch 22 situation. No one wants to fund you until you show success, but you need the money to get to the competitions in order to win and be successful. It's expensive to travel from one place to another. It really is hard, you worry about getting the money to get to the next event, you want to train and prepare, but these things at home can cause you heartache and affect your mental and physical preparation. If you've got no money or have problems at home it's very hard to prepare properly

And preparation really is everything, in every way. For example, there's a chap in the UFC at the moment called Conor McGregor. Irish fighter, uses a combination of Karate, kickboxing and Jujitsu. He's bloody good. He knows it too, as well, and could be accused of working harder selling a fight than he does in the cage. I think that's more the management than him though. He's a fighter, through and through.

I mention Conor here because he's made a lot of waves in

the MMA world by employing a movement coach. A lot of his critics cite this as pretentious or pointless but it really isn't.

I had one.

He was an ex gymnast. A lot of people said 'he's sponging off you and using you', but frankly, I was using him just as much. I have to give him credit, he really helped me to develop a physical programme and to see it through. He didn't know a thing about Judo but he did know how to teach body control and movement, and he helped me, in that respect, immensely. He wasn't alone either, I had many coaches for different things, and that's really the secret to success in any sport, especially Judo; learn from everyone you can.

And I needed a lot of help, because I was in a very odd position. I was a 16 year old kid but I wasn't a normal kid, because at that age I was able to fight the men straight on. That's what impressed Brian Jacks, who was everybody's hero at that point, that I could go toe to toe with the grown men, even though I maybe didn't look like I could. Brian was a huge influence on me when I moved down to London. He was the first World Olympic Medallist in the sport from Britain and his welcome when I showed up at the club was to strangle me unconscious! When I woke up I told him 'You'll never do that again! NEVER!' and I meant it. He could have hit me in the head with a plank and I'd have kept coming for him. As a matter of course, that situation ended up flipping. Inside a few years, Brian was more and more reluctant to train with me. I guess that meant I was getting better.

But before that he taught me a lot about the fundamentals of Judo, especially gripping.

Which brings us to the Judogi, or Gi for short. Judokas know that the Gi, the funny old pyjama jacket, looks a little like a tight fitting robe. But here's the thing; it's our only equipment, our only weapon. If we don't have that jacket then we can't grip up. If we can't grip up we can't throw. Look at any Judo bout at any level and you'll see how much offense is based on control and manipulation of that jacket and, in turn, on the grips we take on it. So Brian helped me immensely and I got a lot of gripping skills from him. Not to mention the tenacity to refuse to stop fighting until I'd beaten him.

That was a crucible in my life. I wasn't just poor and working harder than I ever had; I was a very young boy, especially with regard to my emotions. I had special dispensation to train with the UK team because they saw potential in me. That was great but it meant I was under the spotlight from the start. It was mentally exhausting, being a kid surrounded by these incredibly talented, tough fighters and at first, not being able to defend myself properly. The frustration was constant; going from top banana/cream of the crop at one club to one of the fodder with potential at another.

Looking back I'm amazed at the pressure I was under. We see similar situations now, with certain athletes that are pushed through clubs into national squads at an early age. If it's not directed in the right way it can fail miserably and they stop too early, find other interests. We have to get that foundation in early, teach them how to cope with distractions, how to hone their talent, and turning things into positive outcomes. Most importantly, we have to get them used to not just winning but learning from losing. You have to teach beginners early on in the process, that you can learn from defeat, sometimes a little more than from victory and then you bounce back a better person.

Of course I had no idea about all this when I got to London. But, after a while, I got to the point where I realised I needed help. Somebody to help me prepare from a physical point of view and someone to help me prepare from a psychological point of view. I needed the group we had – which was a world class group with Olympic and World medallists and European Champions. There were a lot of people there who I looked up to and they were my training partners. I had to get the best, get a team around me because as a kid my father was my biggest influence, and with him at a distance, I needed people I could look to for the proper advice and who would support me. Which is where my movement coach and the other members of the team came in. I was at that club 20 years in the end. I made Chief Instructor. That still makes me proud to be a part of such an institution.

It's all about building base, foundation. A good team, good coaches, a good, well rounded skill base. If you haven't got the foundations there, it crumbles. When I look back – I always talk about my father and the foundation he laid because it made a massive difference. It's one of the reasons I won my first British Championships at 10 years of age having started at 7. So all the way through I kept up that consistency because I had that foundation.

A huge part of that was training diaries. One of the coaches I had told me about them and it really helped turn me around. I wrote down things, which were important to me, and sometimes when I look back at the diaries it was nonsense! But as I began to understand the importance of a training diary I realised how I could prepare for events and how I was developing physically. Training and the physical part was more important to me than the mental part. A little bit later on I realised the mental part was probably the most important.

I was also lucky enough to do a lot of international training camps and that gave me a really well rounded perspective on the sport. I went to Japan for months at a time and used a lot of the coaches in Japan to help me develop from a technical point of view.

That meant I stole a lot of ideas. And most coaches and athletes should be if they're doing their jobs right. Plus, stealing a technique is a start, and nothing more. Everything I stole, I evolved. I still do it now. I can look at something, assess it and think of half a dozen ways to use it. On the mat, that made me very dangerous. I can still look at an opponent and know everything they're going to do or try just from how they move. I know if I'm going to throw them inside 10 seconds and I know if I'm in for the fight of my life.

The one arena I wasn't good in at that time was politics. That really became apparent during the run up to the 1980 Olympic Games. Remember the Cold War was at its height then and Russia and many other Eastern European countries boycotted the Games. That was down to the situation in Afghanistan, and Russia's refusal to accept what they were doing there. It was immensely dangerous and controversial.

None of which registered in the mind of a very young, very focused and more than a little, naïve Judoka.

I remember we went into a television studio to film a programme about how America was out of the Olympic Games. Looking back I think 'Damn! I wish I'd been prepared for that question'. I wasn't media prepared at all, but when I do look back now, I still think there's no way they should've stopped us going to the Olympic Games. That wasn't the way to stop the situation and shouldn't have been played by politicians. I just wanted to go to the Olympic Games, and I would've gone if I had to walk there. And we did, we went there representing IOC in the end. It wasn't representing GB, which again I think was wrong, as it was heartbreaking. The politicians will say differently, but you don't get many chances to go to an Olympic Games, most people only get one, if you're lucky you get two and if you're absolutely on top of your game, or you have the tenacity, you get three.

But, political naiveté aside, I was lucky, especially with how I was able to go to Japan. British Judo and the Sports Aid Foundation paid for that. Even now that's not the case for everyone. Small countries have to find their flights or accommodation to get to these events, so they can't afford to do some, or the same amount of events as the fighters at the top. The ones at the top are the ones who have got it easy and able to get to everything, the others find it difficult. Again, it's a catch 22 scenario and to this day I'm glad it's one I was able to avoid, for the most part.

Japan itself was amazing. I went for the first time at aged 16 and I was like a kid in a sweet shop. I was cocky too. There was a guy who we dubbed Gold Tooth as he had a capped tooth. He was a third year student and this guy, he was really good. There's a lot of people in Japan that never do competitions outside of Japan who could easily get medals in World Championships, such is the depth of the country, and this guy was that kind of good! He gave me such a touch when I was there, but, like with Jacks, I kept getting up and I kept coming back at him. I was talking to him under my breath saying 'I'm gonna come back for you and be your nightmare, I'm gonna be there for you every year. I'll hunt you down'. He was horrible, not a very nice man and I remembered him for that. Must have made an impression if I'm still talking about him 40 odd years later!

We went to Japan every six months and so, and I kept looking for him every time. It wasn't until two years later, I found him. I was 18 at that point and I now was a European senior medallist, European champion and a world medallist. I was two years stronger, two years more experienced and I wanted to absolutely crush him. I wanted to knock that gold tooth out of his smiling head. He was still strong but I was relentless. I was gaining on him, getting better each time. It was a year later when I was contending the world title I then became his nightmare! I wouldn't let him go. And oh he wanted to go… far away from me. But I wouldn't let him. It wasn't only because I wanted to dominate him, show him finally who's boss, but as well I didn't think he was a nice person, he was an arse, more than anything he was a bully. I just wanted to put him down. I remember arm locking him and holding him a bit harder than perhaps I should. But it was from the heart and I got him in the end.

A quick aside; and hopefully not too late, Judo is a martial art, and it is a sport that's based entirely around combat. The emotional and psychological highs and lows are higher in combat sports than anywhere else, I'd argue. So while this sounds like it was very intense and violent, and it was, it was also one of the happiest times of my life. My nickname in Japan was 'Happo Bigin', which for years I thought meant 'Happy big 'un'. It actually means 'everybody's friend.' Which is also nice. (*smirk*)

That still makes me smile, years later. Judo is a family and it can be fractious and divided like all families but we all come from the same place and we're all on the same journey.

A big part of that journey, certainly on the mat, is the need to be well rounded.

Judo is derived from the traditional Ju Jitsu, which is a samurai warrior art, but as its English translation will tell you, The Gentle Way, we're more combatants or fighters than killers. There are no strikes whatsoever, instead you grapple with an opponent using their Judogi (jacket) for leverage like I mentioned earlier.

There are four ways of winning: throwing full on to the back, arm locking, strangling for submission or holding down. So three of the ways of winning are on the ground. But we have a massive throwing element to Judo, which makes us different to Brazilian Ju Jitsu, which is so popular thanks to the UFC, and is primarily ground fighting. I'd say that all the way through my career I was probably 70% standing and 30% ground, so I didn't specialise on the ground then at all.

In 1978 I fought a Frenchman named Gilbert when I was going up into the next weight category to get more and harder fights. I fought the British Open in the higher weight category and got to the final easily enough, and there fought Gilbert. He turned me, and strangled me. I left that mat shaking my head and saying 'I would never lose on the ground in international competition again'.

From that moment on I was on a mission. I was look-ing for different moves to specialise in and a friend of mine, Alexander Yatskevich, had this great arm lock. When I started to work through it, I found I had my own way, which was dif-ferent to his and I just worked it. I worked it and drilled it so hard, I was relentless in the way I trained it and approached it. The thing about me is once I start practicing something I had the bottle to do it at competitions - a lot of people will only do it in practice. And I very quickly started to win contests with it.

I worked it so that every time we transitioned from standing down into ground I was ready. I had pulled my ground work up to the same level as my standing game. I just changed the balance. I was working towards taking all risk of chance out of the game plan; to make myself fully adaptable to any situation that presented itself within the match. It won me a lot of contests, lots of major tournaments, it won me the world title, because I transitioned from standing down into ground really well. I drilled it like there was no tomorrow.

If I couldn't catch them on the ground I would throw them and if I couldn't throw them I'd go down to ground. And sometimes, the odd time, I'd play the game, and here we are talking about tactics. I'm known for arm locking or throwing but if I had to play a tactical match and win by putting my backside an inch off the floor, and doing what Mayweather did against Pacquiao, I would do it. Sometimes it was about winning the game. But it always was, and always will, be about learning the game. That was a lesson I was taught early and one that's guided me for decades.

Neil in the zone matside

3. Preparation is Key and the '84 Olympics

Being a pioneer is very difficult. They're the ones that are remembered but they're also the ones who get a lot of push back. People are wary of you being a pioneer, they want to control it, your ideas, and in fact, you. There's this constant conflict between wanting to ride your coattails or use them to drag you down.

But the thing is, and a Judoka knows this better than anyone else, everyone falls eventually. And when this happens, metaphorically or literally, you need to be able to fall properly. You are able to tackle the problem better equipped with the past experience and with a mindful way forward.

That's what we want. That's what competition taught me, to embrace the struggle because you know full well that coming out the other side of it, it's going to be you winning and the other guy licking his wounds.
That doesn't mean it isn't terrifying of course.

I get asked about nerves a lot. If I ever got nervous before competition. I get very nervous, at every level of working in this sport. I'll get nervous before a demonstration or a presentation. I'll get nervous before going on to do a kids' seminar!

But I get better as I get closer to the presentation, so I get less nervous as I'm preparing. The harder I prep for it, and the better I prep for it, the easier I am in my mind, so a lot of it is down to the preparation. It doesn't matter if I am presenting to kids or to coaches, whether I am presenting it to a national body or whether I am competing at the Olympic Games, or British Championship, whatever it is, I get nervous but as the event draws closer, I get better at coping with it. Nerves turn to anticipation.

When I think back to the Olympic Games I think about what I call the 'tunnel syndrome'. There's nothing more terrifying than stepping into that tunnel, with the lights dimming, and it closes in on you. I remember being with my coach Tony McConnell at the 1980 Olympic Games. He would do anything to get my mind to think about different things. We were talking about garden gnomes at one point, gardening and just everyday things and he said: 'if you weren't here now, where would you be?' I said 'in my garden' and we were talking about weeding, my mum shouting out 'do you want a cup of tea?', and yeah, those gnomes. I don't know why gnomes. I've never owned a garden gnome in my life!

It was just nonsense, I was about to go on the mat to fight for the Olympic title, it was bizarre but it took my mind off what I was there for. Then Whamo! All of a sudden it's Neil Adams, not the gardener, but the Judoka, and then it's game on!

I remember I had to step up on a platform; my legs were giving way, but as I stepped up I got stronger and the crowd were there shouting for both parties. I grew stronger as I got nearer to it.

Then they shouted 'HAJIME!' which is 'begin' and we were away.

Had I done the preparation right? Could I have done certain things better? I know *now* that I could have done things better as far as my diet in the 1980 Games. It's a hard pill to swallow now, looking back as you think you are in complete control of everything, and I was, Judo-wise. I had technically prepared, I had researched all my opponents, knew them inside and out. I had phased my training properly. However, as far as being a 'pioneer', I wasn't up to par on sports nutrition. And this is what inevitably let me down. The decision was to either maintain my ranking in the lower weight of u71kg or to stay in the higher weight of u78kg where I had been fighting all year, and winning. Ultimately, my decision was based on calculated risk, or so I thought at the time, that the one thing I couldn't control was the draw, so to eliminate or reduce that risk was to maintain my ranking position in the lower weight. What I didn't count for was the absolute agony of cutting that weight and the physical affect it would have on me. Ezio Gamba was (and is) a very tactical fighter and would have exploited every crack in the armour he would have found. He was half a step ahead of me the whole fight and there are few things more awful for a competitor than feeling a fight go away from you. The harder you try to get it back, the further it goes away. The more you claw, the more your attempts are futile, ill placed and ultimately ineffective.

The 1984 Olympics were different. I had everything there physically, I was the right weight, I knew I was technically superior, but I was mentally tired, really exhausted and I think it was because I was the favourite that I felt the pressure even more.

As I was World Champion in '81, and was world silver medallist in '83 on a split decision, I was still top ranked in the world going into '84 as one of the favourites to win the Olympic gold medal. My preparation had gone well however, I couldn't shake the tiredness. Like my mojo wasn't quite where it should be. In comparison to the 1980 Games for example, there I flew through the tournament, which was lucky as the final took all I had and then some. In 1984, the tournament didn't go my way at all. Every fight was a struggle and I had to really pull it out the bag for each one. I was just slightly off kilter and I didn't really know why. I fought Michel Nowak, who I had fought many times, he was physically one of the strongest men I had to fight, ever. I was relying on him tiring in the second part of the contest, as he had done on the previous match ups. I used to train with a focus on my muscular endurance, especially for fighters like him. I'd wait for the 3 minutes mark then I'd pick up the pace in order to pull him in. In other matches he'd start to lose gas. But, when I faced him at the '84 Olympic Games quarter finals, he just came on coming and coming. I was thinking 'oh my God! Where is he getting this endurance from all of sudden?' I just managed to score on him, therefore just managing to come through into the semi final.

The semi-final was again fighting someone I had beaten five times before and each time I had beaten him by Ippon - Judo's equivalent to a knock out. This match again was hard work for me; I was winning, just not as clearly as I would have liked. So, I was in the final but it had been harder work than I would have liked and really, expected. I remember I was beside the mat, and I was coming down into that tunnel thinking, 'I just can't wait for it to end'. I had a different approach to this Games, I just wanted it over. Then I could rest! I could have a break. Maybe do something a bit different.

It was the final, I was ready to go on. I was fighting a German (Frank Wieneke) who wasn't even ranked in these Games as he was a relative new comer and I'd beaten him in the European Championships a month earlier. So really, I thought I had nothing to worry about. Even though I wasn't on top form I could still win this match and be Olympic Champion. I was stepping up with a different mind set than in 1980, because in 1980 I was at the start of my career and in 1984 I was contemplating retirement from competition. It made a difference. I was hungry for it, but was I hungry for IT, the Gold medal, or was I hungrier for it to be over and done with? Were the nerves I was feeling trying to tell me something? To bring me into focus? Or was it a premonition of sorts, knowing deep, deep down I wasn't as on point or prepared as I wanted to be, knew I should be.

A big part of fighting nerves is something obvious and linked to preparation that not near enough athletes at any level do; and that is the warm up. I can't say enough to athletes about just how important the warm up is before major events – any event, I don't care what it is, and it is the last thing you want do, I know. Nobody likes to warm up, so they skim over it. Just get enough of a sweat on. 'Don't want to use up energy or get tired out,' they'll say. But the top champions and even the top singers and performers – they all warm up. They are in their changing rooms or warm up areas doing it and doing it 100%. It is an absolute skill that is missed by many Judokas and can turn their day around if done properly.

In a situation like that you get what some actors call 'pre-performance fatigue'. You just want to sit down and think 'I'll be alright, I'll be fine'. And you will too, once you warm up and get moving and keep moving.

Here's how I did it. Before the '80 and '84 Olympics fights I had the equivalent of an Olympic final in the training area, it was the hardest contest - in the training area with my partner – having to go through the process of taking your heart rate to over 150 – 160bpm. Physically you feel dead, you want to lie down and sleep. When you are nervous or frightened you want to sleep, you want it to go away. Did you ever notice that you yawn a lot coming up to fights? That's your body telling you that you need oxygen, that your brain needs oxygen and this is because nerves are expending that very energy you are trying to conserve. The warm up wakes you up and gets that much needed oxygen to the brain and muscles.

It never goes away either. I've had times since, when I've been nervous, absolutely terrified, and yet I've thought 'you did the Olympic Games and World Championships, and you have had to cope with it. You can cope with this, damn it!'.

For my preparation for the '81 World Championships when I won against Jiro Kase from Japan, I had perfect training and preparation. I knew I was going to beat him. I don't think I have felt that feeling again to be honest. Every bone, sinew, muscle, tooth and hair knew I had this. That was a great feeling, I couldn't go wrong, I knew I wasn't going to lose!

There's a downside to that level of preparation and focus and it's something I found when I reread my old book. You're hard to live with, self-centred and thinking only of yourself – maybe self-absorbed is a better word?

In the book, I come across as arrogant, because back then, quite frankly, I was. I was selfish, and I was very focused coming up to 1980- 1984. That meant I had only one thing on my mind and it was all about me and where I needed to be. Saying that, I didn't like being alone either.

I was in a relationship with a lady named Helen at the time. She is, tragically, no longer with us. She was lovely but we were both young and I was on a mission. We got engaged, because you're at that age where you think you're expected to but it was not the right time for either of us.

When I got back from the Olympic Games we split up and that's when I met Sharron Davies. Sharron was another Olympian and, now, we get on really well. At the time? We clashed a lot.

Sharron and I got together at an awards dinner, it was great because cameras were there and all the glamour that went with it. I liked that. I felt pretty cool and with that flow of energy and attention it didn't take long for us to become an item, and Britain's Press Darlings.

Now, take my mindset at the time; entirely focused, completely self-centred, utterly dedicated to being the best athlete I could be at any expense, whatsoever.

Multiply that by two, because Sharron was exactly the same.

Then, put us together. It could only be volatile.

So there we were; two Olympians, two entirely driven people and one of us was tall, glamorous and blonde.

And that one was not me.

Then I hated it. I hated being second fiddle, not just in the relationship but in how we were reviewed. It started to affect my preparation for events and of course I couldn't have that, so, in the end, we split up. Plus we were both young and wanted to live our lives on our own terms, expecting the other to just fall in. Well that was never going to happen on either side. Besides, we were getting in each other's way. I resented her attention to a degree and she, when I won the World and European Championships resented mine, so it was best all around for us to go our separate ways. She retired not long after the 1980 Olympics and I think her early retirement affected us both more than we thought at the time. It was a crossroads, in every sense.

Relationships are the toughest part of being a professional athlete. Sharron and I were too alike in our focus and self-absorbing ways to be healthy. I can assume that the thing that attracted her to me the most was my 'winning ways' but which would turn out to be the thing she hated most when she retired before me. And with both Helen and Alison, my first wife, who I married after the 1984 Olympics, their genuine attempts to support me were made more difficult by me and my absolute focus on winning. I was high maintenance. However, they didn't, they couldn't, understand where I was at that point. I couldn't communicate with them on that level as they just weren't there. You don't know what you don't know.

It's such a thin line to walk; go too far in one direction you're in the way. Go too far in the other you don't care. We're tough people to live with.

That's one of the many, many reasons I'm so lucky with Niki, my second wife who I met in Sydney at the 2000 Games. We have an idyllic marriage, like my parents have. We're both Olympic athletes, we've both competed, but instead of it being our lives, it's our job.

We don't let Judo dictate our lives, or at least we try not to and have interests other than the sport that we do together and we have our family, so we don't let Judo rule. Also, we haven't got the pressure of competitions and we often say now we don't know how it would've been if I'd been her coach, because I'd have been a hard coach, a hard task master. On the sly, I think I could've got more out of her competition days, but that's another story for another day.

It can work really well – you have to come to a compromise and if you don't come to some compromise – like any marriage, you're going to clash. It's important you work out between you how it's going to work. You would think having someone there is much needed support. Certainly for me having somebody there, at home while I prepared for the '80 Olympic Games didn't really help me at the time – hands up, a lot of that was me. I was selfish and directed and determined, nothing was going to stop me reaching my goals.

Coming up to '84 I started to change my mentality and consider other things that were going to be part of my life, it wasn't just going to be about Judo. Because if I had won the gold medal I was possibly going to retire from competition, so I was looking beyond the competition side of things. I was looking for something else.

Neil at the '88 Games

4. The '88 Question

At the end of the 1984 Olympic Games I was really tired. Physically I was exhausted and mentally I needed a rest. It's easy to talk about retirement when you're weary and in need of a time out, but often after reflection the reality is somewhat different. Even before I turned to close scrutiny of why and how I lost the Olympic title and recuperating physically and mentally the question that I asked myself was:

Have I got another Olympic games in me?

Followed by another:

If not, what I am going to do?

The logical choice was coaching because so many athletes go into coaching after competition. For me, it was a necessity. I hadn't gone to study and received a higher education that guided me anywhere else positively, and Judo was the most important thing in my life. So, coaching looked likely. I was still in good shape, so I was hovering a little. In the two weeks following the Games, I married Alison. It was a new path in a different direction. After that, and our honeymoon, I would see what direction things went in after that.

So, a couple of weeks passed and… well… what was always going to happen happened. I decided I didn't want to leave it there. I decided I had more in the tank. So I decided I was going to train up for the German Open. I was going to hunt down Wieneke.

The German Open was 6-8 weeks after the Olympic Games and I just carried on training. I was tired mentally but I didn't stop. We've talked elsewhere about how difficult it is when you're obsessed with something and I was. I had unfinished business. What I really wanted was to meet Wieneke and to lay the ghost of the Olympics. So there I was, in the German Open when I met a fighter called Legień from Poland who was later to become 2 times Olympic Champion. This was the first of three matches that I was going to have with him in 1984/85 at different tournaments. I fought him and beat him in the semi-final. Then I had Wieneke and he actually gave me a much better match in the German Open. In the Olympic final, I was way ahead of him and only had made an error of judgement to lose that title. At the Olympics, me relaxing at the safety area for the split second was all it took for him to find his opening, throwing himself in for the attack that would seal the deal. This time however, at the German Open, he was the Olympic Champion and in his home country and all the pressure was on him, but he used it effectively and fought very, very well.

I just won it, I got the decision.

Did it lay it to rest?

No.

A decision win was never going to do it. I couldn't feel satisfied with myself with that and when the press went straight to him after the fight that just confirmed it. I'd won but it didn't matter. Because I hadn't won at the Olympics.

I knew why too, and in all honesty so did he. I got ahead of myself in that fight, he took the opportunity and quite right too, I'd have done the same. The weird thing is, by losing in the German Open his stock actually rose at home. The German press had been saying it was a fluke but actually because he gave me a good fight in the German Open, they said it wasn't a fluke and that he was up there with the greats.

So, again, I'd won. But it didn't matter. A shadow was forming, a deep-seeded ball of doubt and for the first time ever in my life, insecurity. But, of course, I carried on training. It's what I knew to do. It was all that was familiar to me. Even though at that point I still hadn't decided if I was going to another Olympics or not.

Next up was the 1985 European Championships in April. Training for it was hard. Not so much because of fitness, I was coming off training camps for the World Championships, but because I'd just got married in August. My routine had completely changed, my life had changed with it and those changes made it very difficult to focus. This wasn't just an engagement or two people living together. I was married. I had to start thinking of two of us now.

Plus there was the fact I'd wanted to finish in 1984 and yet, here I was. I was on the back of a major upset, losing the Olympic Title and a win in Germany that was suppose to make it all better, but didn't. I was still training hard, I always do but I was... depleted. My psychology wasn't right, my mind wasn't sharp because I'd planned to finish in 1984. That first question hadn't gone away either:

Have I got another Olympic Games in me?

I just didn't know.

I went anyway.

It's something I see so often now. Fighters who take one step too far and you can see it's gone, they've gone. It's not just a physical thing, your body doesn't just suddenly crack.

That's a progressive thing. It's emotional and mental. When they say its 90% mental application, it is! If your mind isn't there 100% it's going to affect your preparation and that's exactly what happened.

So, my life had changed completely. I'd decided to retire and yet I was still training and competing. That leads us to another, simple question with a very complicated answer.

Why?

Unfinished business. Worse, the sense of a job being left undone. Let me give you an example from non-competitive life; A little while ago, a young lad came in to paint my fence. My girls and I were standing in front of the finished product and even my girls said 'you're not happy with that Dad are you' and I wasn't. And they weren't, so in the end my daughter said 'if you pay me, I'll do it'.

I told her, 'it has to be done properly: no lines, the edges doing, it has to be done properly'.

That sense of perfection that is needed for a job to not just be done for the sake of being done, but done right, is something I get from my dad. He was a master carpenter, and had an eye for precision. He'd finish the job and taught me that the eye is always drawn to the gap, not the good bits you've done. So for me, in my Judo career, there were gaps that needed filling. I did not complete the task that I'd set myself and that was what drove me, thinking 'I have to dig in and complete this'.

Or to put it another way:

Have I got another Olympic Games in me?

My answer might have been different if it was now, because presently you have to qualify through world ranking points. Back then we could qualify through our Country alone. But back then it was a situation where I had to be ahead of my British opponents to go to these Olympic Games. Make no mistake, I would always have had a chance to qualify because I was fighting at that level over a period of 12 years and I was always consistent. Even though I was back with the pack and not way ahead as I was in previous Olympic build ups, I still had the level to go through to another Olympic Games, however, with new management, the big question now was: would I be selected?

Even that was weird though. I'd always been the one that was being chased and now all of a sudden I was the one that was chasing. Saying that, I prepared well and I don't know if it was perfect training, or I had received the rest I needed, but I went to the '85 Europeans and I blitzed everybody. I destroyed the field, threw the Russian in the Semi Final, threw them all bang, bang, bang - and I thought 'Aha! I've still got it'.

5 months after the European Championships we had the World Championships in Korea. We arrived very late so the preparation was an absolute catastrophe. That's not an excuse I'm given her either, more a fact.

It got worse when we got there too. The draw that I had was against Hikage who I had fought in the previous World final in '83. They'd brought him back in '85 and he was the number one ranked competitor as he was still the reigning World Champion from 2 years before. Remember, the World Championships were every two years then, not every year.

I lost the first fight against him by a decision, and then had to work my way through to fight for 3rd place. That was really the hardest day of my competitive life because I fought all the top people, I fought them all, one after another. My timing was off, the room was spinning, I felt dazed because of the time difference and jetlag. That was the hardest bronze medal I've ever won. I won every match but it was hard work and slog. It was the *complete* opposite of the way the Europeans had went and I remember coming away from there thinking 'do I really want to go for this, another 3 years of this?'

Strangely, my answer came through coaching. My coaching experience, at that point, was a little strange. I'd always coached, but I'd always taught individual lessons or techniques. Basically seminars, where I'd come in and demonstrate something and then work with a group as they learned it.

Odd as it sounds, that didn't really prepare me for teaching a group over a period of time. Don't get me wrong; I was a thorough, careful teacher. I was always able to pass on my knowledge but I was aware that my skills were raw and unfocused. It's that fence again, the need to do a job properly if it was going to be done at all. And if I wanted to do this, I needed to add to my experience in teaching. I needed to add a new skills set.

The opportunity came in the form of a job offering. I moved to France to teach at the Racing Club de France – the mecca sports club in France, an all-sports club. They put a lot of money and resources into many sports and Judo was one of their main sports.

My son Ashley was one year old. So while my life had changed again, he was at an age where a move like that wouldn't damage him. So, we upped and moved to Paris for one year with an option to extend the contract if it worked.

It wasn't easy. For a start I hadn't negotiated the contract well enough and so we were living on the outskirts of Paris, meaning I had to commute in every day. Also, this was my first time living in a different country and I wasn't prepared. I went in with a British mindset and was appalled to find that the apartment we moved into didn't have anything in it. No furniture, no appliance, not even any light fittings. I know now they never do but that was a nasty, and expensive, surprise.

It wasn't the only nasty surprise either. I didn't negotiate the car well enough and in the end both the car and the apartment took up most of my wages, so we ended up struggling and there we were on a one year contract. I had a young Labrador called Bob, a one year old and my wife Alison, who was stuck in the apartment, not knowing anybody at all. It was, in a word, miserable. For all of us.

That was on me. This is where I thought I needed to go. The next step. However, I was just so naive in terms of living outside the sports personality bubble, it costs us. Alison was of course supportive but at that point the pressure on us was incredible. We were newly married, new parents, living in a foreign country under far worse conditions than expected. I wasn't calm, but I was definitely calming and I did understand that it wasn't all about me. We'd made a commitment, we had Ashley, obviously wanted the contract, as well as our marriage to work. It was very tough and we did what we could.

As to why France? Well it was really a two for the price of one kind of offer. Not only was it the chance to go out and learn a trade but to coach at one of the largest clubs in France, because France are something of a Judo superpower. They have 1.5 million people doing Judo and they have a fantastic National system that produces Olympic and World Champions all the time. I wanted to learn and soak up all of this.

At one time in the 50's and 60's they were very similar to Great Britain. They were our top rivals in Europe and the world other than Japan. They had some top business guys that really pushed it in a certain ways and developed it, so I wanted to learn their system, I wanted to know how it worked.

I learnt such a lot from their National system and how they had taken Judo forwards. I was developing my own ideas and was learning how to develop them. A big part of what I did at the Racing Club was to open the doors to other clubs for practice purposes. The French mentality at that point was very much to keep it within the club, keep it elite, and I wanted to try it another way.

The whole point of Judo, and on a larger level, fitness, is it's there for everyone. That was one of my big challenges actually. There was a bit of trouble about it, I had to explain myself. I wanted to do it my way for a year or not at all and I think it went very, very well. I wanted to be a fly on the wall and learn and the pay-off was to help some of their athletes. Which of course meant fighting them, something the French were very happy to have me do. Even the ones I fought in the Olympic Games like Michel Nowak, who on top of the Games, I had fought seven times. One of the strongest men I have ever fought in my life. And there he was, and there I was, as his coach. About a month in, he saddled up to me and said 'come on, we can do it, there's nobody watching'. I turned to him in mock shock 'Are you kidding? I've gone 10 years trying to avoid you!'

Michel and I became good friends too which was great. It was also part of the French's willingness to have me train with their top fighters. It made sense, bringing an athlete of my level to train with and compete against their athletes. They actually started sharpening me up. In fact they started generating my interest again and I started to realise that I was still able to fight all these top guys.

They were the ones who pulled me into the office and said 'why don't you go for the next Olympics?' They loved what I was doing there at the Club, but it was crazy. They actually wanted me to fight in one of the French team championships, so of course they had an underlying motive. Great kudos for them and I was the first ever non-French athlete to fight in that team championship. So I decided to go for it and that was the start of my training for the '88 Olympics.

I had my answer.

But with it came some serious consequences.

Neil, with Ashley and Bob, in Paris

5. France and its Consequences

From a professional point of view, France was amazing. I was working with some of the best people there, I'd had a year in France that, professionally, was really beneficial to me.

From a personal point of view, France was a disaster. I knew very early that I didn't want to live in France, and that we'd be coming back to the UK. The family was really unhappy, my dog was miserable, my wife was miserable, even my one year old kid was miserable.

Worse, I was never at home. I was working for the club and they took advantage of that. It was one year of 100% work, which was good for my apprenticeship, and make no mistake, it was an apprenticeship. It was a great chance to look at their system and the way they did things. It gave me ideas as to what I'd do when I was preparing my own students and it also made me look at how to rehash my own teaching methods. And, at the same time, get ready for the next Olympic Games.

I had some competition for the position on the '88 team too. I wasn't the only one who had expected me to bow off after the LA Games. Paul Shields, a terrific man and Judoka was working really hard to qualify for the 1988 Olympic Games and in a lot of ways he was a better prospect than me. Arthur Mapp's view, and he was Team Manager at this point, was that I'd already done two Olympics and didn't need to be part of a third. I was a veteran, and that made me an outsider and when you're Team Manager having somebody there who wasn't quite part of the team is a bit of a distraction so I can understand his position about that in some ways.

Also, I could have behaved better. Looking back I half demanded, expected preferential treatment because of who I was. In some ways it was right, in some ways it was wrong and I think that he would have rather not had to deal with me. Paul would have gone to his first Olympic Games and done his best and who knows? With my coach's head on, my thoughts are that he probably wouldn't have had the same chance that I had, given the experience I held, even though I was on the way down. I was over my peak, but even over my peak I always had the chance of a medal at the Olympics and I thought 'No, if I can qualify for this team, I am going to go'. Like I say, I'd made my decision. People who know me well, know that once my mind's made up, it's very difficult to shake me from it.

So, the Team Manager had his meeting with me and I made my case. I said 'Listen, I'm the number one and I will do everything that I have to do. You tell me what I have to do'. So Arthur set out a number of events that I had to do and I started the preparation all the way up to the Olympics. I was medalling in each and every event that I did. I was getting there.

But it was hard. I was back in the pack, again, biting and clawing to get where I needed to be and honestly, it was horrible. Every combat sport athlete fights themselves every time they compete, and I see it in other guys now. You drop out for a couple of years and when you come back the body isn't quite there but the heart is. You fight harder, you work harder and you trust that what you can't physically do anymore will be covered by what you can mentally do. You fight with your heart and your mind and although they are willing sometimes your body is not. That's what I did. Or tried to do.

I was fighting for my career the whole time, too. If I'd slipped up at any of the junctions, the Manager would have pushed me aside for sure. I have no doubt about that but being the kind of person I am, I kept showing up. That's a lot of what Judo is, persistence. But that persistence can be unforgiving and in the end, Paul found that out.

We were scheduled to meet in one competition and Paul was injured and didn't show. He phoned me a few days after the competition, and asked me to quit, to give up my spot. He said 'listen, this is my dream and man-to-man and friend-to-friend, could you maybe....' and I stopped him.

I said 'I'm sorry, Paul, but if I get selected I'm going, that's what I'm doing'.

There was friction, of course, because he was disappointed but we stayed friends. We still are good friends. A lot of that stems from the fact, I think, that if our roles had been reversed he'd have done the same. Especially being favourite for two Olympic Games and this time coming in as an underdog for a medal. You have to take any chance because if you're not careful you find it's passed you by, and you're sat there thinking 'what am I going to do?' Or worse, 'What if?'

So it was my dream, it was his dream. It was him, or me.

I think about that fight a lot, and what would have happened if Paul and I had had it out. To be quite honest, if I'd lost the match I would have conceded. I knew I was pushing myself, knew I was on thin ice but I kept winning so I kept going. Even my losses were narrow, and one in particular really stuck with me. I was chasing Legien and that was odd, because at the beginning it was him chasing me! I'd lost the decision to him in one of the matches prior to these Olympics and he was the one that became the Olympic champion there, but that one time he was on the back foot. I was winning that match. So, I knew I was still very close, still up there and around and about but just not quite there. I had the eventual Olympic champion off balance so I couldn't have been that far off.

It was a terrible situation to be in. I was under huge professional pressure, my marriage was starting to show strains, but even with all that, I still thought, 'I've got an outside chance here if I get a good draw, if I get just a little bit of luck on my side'. If I could get this all will be well.

That's the brilliant, awful thing. The Olympic Games

create surprises. Sometimes, somehow, even with the system that they've got at the moment where they get all the top seeds there, you'll get someone who delivers an extraordinary performance and wins an Olympic medal. We have seen it many times at the Olympic Games. Hearts are broken and heroes are made. That's what an Olympic Games does - it creates surprises and I wanted this time to be one of those, I wanted a surprise. I needed to be the surprise. Everything seemed to be aligning and giving me that last chance. Or at least that's what I was telling myself.

All this constant training and pressure does nothing but put added strain on your home life. A home life that was already tough due to the issues about the apartment and France. I was definitely not the best person to live with and it became difficult. It was made worse by the fact that a lot of us played as hard as we worked. I would never have a drink or go to parties up to an event but afterwards it was a different ball game and we'd… well we would celebrate, we would celebrate hard. It was great in the short term but inevitably I got to the point where when I was a bit down and I started to drink to take the edge off.

That point was after the '88 Olympics. I prepared hard for those Games but did not attend the same International camps as before because of my family situation, so was not as well prepared as the previous two Games. Now, years later, what we're finding is this is a pretty common pattern for athletes, and adults, who are transitioning from being selfish individuals to a thoughtful family person. It's a difficult process for some, but an important one for all.

But the tunnel was very long. After the '88 Games, I started to train to earn the beer that evening rather than to get better through the training. And, as pressures at home mounted that beer wasn't enough. The Games were done, things had ended badly and our roles had been reversed. I was left with looking after Ashley more while Alison was studying for a degree.

I'm not blaming her for that either, it was a very sensible move. She'd realised, I think long before me, that if everything went pear shaped, which in some ways, competition wise it had, then we needed more avenues for money. Or if the marriage didn't work, what would she do? That time alone in France, I think she realised, for herself what did she have to show for all of this? Nothing. So she decided that she really needed to do something that would make her independent. She was a very focused person, so she decided to do the University degree.

She didn't want to just pass the degree, she wanted to get a 1st and she wanted to be the best. So for a three year period, it was very much me on my own in the evenings with Ashley. He and I would do things as she studied. More and more we did things apart as she concentrated on her school work and I concentrated on Ashley. More and more we started to see a crack in our relationship.

As years went on; I was doing the family thing and still trying to train as I usually did and it wasn't happening. I didn't train the same as I used to. Now that I wasn't competing, I was training only for my physical condition. It was difficult for both of us really and I realise now, I was always looking for something particular within a relationship and never realised what it was until 16 years ago when I met Niki. Now, things are amazing and I've found what I was looking for. A relationship is work, you will always have to work at it. What it shouldn't be is *hard* work. You should wake up looking forward to sharing the day with that person, wondering what the first thing will be that you will laugh about. To feel the passion so much that you don't want to get out bed to go to work and stay right where you are.

Looking back Alison and I had a relationship that was not working in the same way. The honeymoon bubble had burst, we were in a foreign country, and we were only really starting to get to know each other, not only as new parents, but as people, as our courtship and engagement was quick by normal standards. However, we weren't going to realise this, really, until once the Games were over. Maybe we needed a little more time together before getting married rather than marrying directly after the '84 Games.

Don't get me wrong, we were and still are friends but there was something more that we both needed and it just wasn't there. I think we both realised that. That yes, friends, and someone who I care about and what happens to them, but just not that spark, that all encompassing need to be linked to that person. I guess some would call it passion. I looked for it in Judo, she looked for it in studying and I think we both realised we weren't finding it in each other.

Externally, I was in good physical shape. Inside, I was not very healthy and becoming unhealthier. I started hiding the drinking and, because no one's ever good at that, I got caught a couple of times. That caused even more tension between Alison and myself and, in the end she didn't know what to do with the situation and neither did I. I knew what I was doing was wrong. Why else would I feel the need to hide it? I also knew deep down that I needed to get control, I knew in my mind that I could and would get control of it, but somehow I always put it off to the next day. I knew I was doing it, but I didn't stop. I couldn't; it wasn't the right time. But then again, it was never the right time.

Neil fighting Nevzerov

6. Hunting and Hunted

I was chasing that medal from the age of 17. That ever-elusive Olympic Gold medal could have, would have, should have… been mine. It was all I ever wanted, really.

I fought the 1976 Olympic champion, a great Champion called Vladimir Nevzerov, in Moscow and I scared him. I got close to him, I knew this was something I didn't just want to do, I *COULD* do it.

I was a good hunter. Because that's what you are when you are trying to get to the top, a hunter chasing the title. But when I got the World Champion title myself I realised that my role had changed. I wasn't hunting anymore. I was the prey.

You are a different person. I went from being the chaser – I was always chasing, chasing from 17 years of age in that match against Nevzerov and I then went all over the World trying to get a match against him. And I gave him a scare in that 1977 Senior European Championships. I got close to him and looking back I think, possibly, it forged his decision to retire from competition. In those early days, I was chasing Nevzerov, and then in 1984/5 Waldemar Legień was chasing me. Wherever I was, he'd be there at the same event – he was doing what I did, chasing me as I was the best at the time and he wanted it. I fought him 3 times in 1985: once in the German Open, in the final of the European Championships and then for 3rd place at the World Championships. He was on me the whole time.

So being the chaser, and being the one chased are two different things. I was the Number 1 in the world and was the one to be knocked off the pedestal. It's always hard if you are the number one, you have to make a mental and physical adjustment. That's when being consistent in your performances and mind set is such an advantage. Later on before I retired, I found myself as the chaser again, trying to get my level back up to where I was. I look at it like road cycling. In a race, you get one or two that break away and the others are the chasing pack – and sometimes they pull the pack back. I was back in the pack trying to be the number one again. For 10 years I was out there ahead of the pack and found that being one of the chasers was more than hard work. It was soul destroying.

It gets harder as you get not even older, but more experienced too. I found that when I was preparing for '88. It's a great idea making comebacks when you're in the bar, everybody sat there 'round the table, and people say 'you're still young, you can still do this, you can do the next one' – you think 'yeah you're right!' But then in training it's two different things, you think, 'was this a good idea?' A great idea in the bar, but in reality, not always so great.

I had a conversation with Ilias Iliadis - a great champion,

he was World Champion in 2014 and Olympic Champion in 2004 so it's a 10 year period as a great champion. He wants to go to his last Olympics in Rio but it's a different preparation for this one. He is aware that he is not preparing the same as the other competitions. I said to him 'you know what, you have to look at your training and your competitions, because you have to do this one differently'. This cannot be done the same as the others. He is now 29 years of age, not 18 anymore and he has a wife and 2 kids. You've got a different body, who are carrying injuries who didn't have starting out, and that means that your mental application and other responsibilities change your whole concept of preparation. Being a great Champion will always give him the chance to medal but at some stage we have to accept that things have changed and they continue to change throughout your life.

That's even truer once you stop competing. To me, being the best isn't enough. The truly great athletes and great people are remembered for other things that go with it. So just winning the event is one thing but how you carry that forward or pass that on is even more important. It's about being humble, respectful. And yes, of course it is about winning, and I'm the self-professed worst loser in the world, but it's how you cope with that, how you are with your opponent, how you respect them and how they feel. People notice how you react, win or lose and we need to teach the younger generation that larger framework of respect if we want the sport to thrive.

Of course you still have to deal with that loss yourself. Mine still haunt me. Niki will tell you it's hard sleeping next to somebody that has the same reoccurring dream all the time, or maybe nightmare is the better word, and I get quite physical within the dream. It's still there, its unfinished business. The mare can go from me having another chance at winning the Olympic gold medals: I'm out there, I'm just about to do it, but I can't quite get to the mat area on time, or I'm late or there's something to do with the training arrangements to get there and every time something goes wrong, it doesn't ever quite happen.

Niki brought it to light one morning when recounting my dream to her, she said,

'it's strange that you have that same kind of dream. It doesn't take too much to see that you've got something to work out in there, and then maybe there' She pointed to my head and then to my heart.

It's not always at the Olympic Games either, it could be me giving a lecture or seminar and I don't quite get there on time. I used to be late all the time in my early years until my training partner at the time called me on it. He took me to one side and pointed out he was always there on time for me, and found that he was always waiting for me as well. It also took Sid Hoare to say that he wouldn't employ me; that I was always late.

He also said to me, 'that shit sticks.'

At first, I thought it was just people having a go at me, but then I stopped and had a really good think about it. I really took what these people had said to heart and decided to do something about it. So, for years now, I'm on time. And Sid was right, that shit does stick as I still get people surprised to see me early to things, still expecting me to be late, based on the reputation I had back then.

It's like a bereavement, because I can look at the good things and think 'I did great, I was a pioneer. I took it somewhere. I was the first men's World champion from Great Britain ever, the first one to break the Japanese dominance in the middle weights in the whole world'. I broke barriers and that one I'll never forget. The two Olympic silvers though are unfinished business. I've coped with it, to a degree, and I can smile about it now – it just may look like gritted teeth from time to time.

One of the things about Judo in particular is that your choices outside of the fight matter as much as your choices inside. I realise that now and see it quite clearly from my commentary position. People notice if you walk away in a huff, or worse, from a match or an opponent. If you lose and walk away, or you say something offensive or kick a chair, people will remember that.

Conversely, Anton Geesink, the first man to break the barriers beating the Japanese at their own game in the 1964 Tokyo Olympic Games knew that. He beat the Japanese champion in the final and the Dutch team wanted to swarm the mat and lift him up into the air. Geesink stopped them, out of respect for Kaminaga who he had just beaten. He bowed respectfully and left the mat in an orderly way. The Japanese never forgot that. Neither have I.

So people remember you on how you are, how you behave. There are certain things people will remember me for fondly and others where I did not handle the situation well. That means I'll be remembered for some of the wrong reasons in some cases but I have learnt from my mistakes. Being humble costs nothing.

I've always tried to be the better person, on and off the mat. You don't have to be an arse. We can be determined and directed and we can even hate losing but how we pre-sent ourselves win or lose is the key. Like the being on time bit, it might seem a very small thing to some people but it's massive to others. It does demonstrate respect for the other person and their time. In life, time keeping is one of the more important things you have to adhere to, you turn up late for your job, they'll sack you. And you lose respect if you're late. A very simple thing to control– your clock! Make an effort, don't let people down, it makes a difference and people will remember. If you are true to your word people respect that.

I watch a lot of athletes approaching these milestones and I see how it is for them and I know how hard that is. You know physically – ok well in actually fact, physically I was able to still fight a lot of the top fighters up to 40 years of age in training camps etc. In the dojo you can still be very good, but outside the dojo, when you get into the competi-tion arena you realise that you have lost the hunger for it, you have other priorities in your life. I watch athletes coming to the stage in their life, where they want to change direction – it's normally in about 10 year increments - and I watch some who can't let it go or they are finding it hard to accept it. I've been there, done that. Have the T-shirt... actually, a few of them to be fair.

Realising that is devastating in itself. I talked to an athlete friend and I asked 'what do you miss most about competition?'

And he said 'the simplicity of life'. It's simple, it's easy. You don't have to think too much outside the box as you have one job and one job only. You turn up, you train, you do competition, you come back, you rest, you eat, you drink, you prepare... that's what the athletes are doing. They're leading a great life. It's not all beer and skittles going from one place to another but actually it's easier than the alternative: bills, mortgage, school fees, car payments – at the elite level, those who are funded, they have a good life, they see the world, and a lot of them get money now to do that. The simplicity is what you lose because all of a sudden there are other things you have to consider: your partner, your kids, where your next meal is coming from, where your next set of trainers come from! I remember the first time I had to purchase a new set of trainers from, yes- a store, and turning to the salesperson, mouth gaping open, asking 'How much?!' And as soon as you become responsible for others, your life changes. The sooner you recognise that, the better.

The old Coventry Judo Club

7. The Ends

As I said, I went into the Olympic Games in 1988 not as physically prepared as I was for the previous two. I hadn't done the same amount of time in Japan that I had done before and that meant that I hadn't done the amount of sparring that I normally did prior to a major competition. I had slight problems at home, the blush of new romance had faded slightly, which was niggling at me and affecting me mentally, so when you look at it like that, it was not the ideal preparation for an Olympics. So going to Korea in '88 I realised that things had to change when I got back home. My relationship with Alison was not as great as I thought or wanted it to be, and I had finished my final competition with an unsatisfactory performance.

A lot of sports are lonely, combat sports in particular. It's a very odd feeling stepping onto that mat alone but almost every time I did, I thought I was going to leave the winner. Even from '84-'88, even in the middle of everything that was happening, I was hoping for a miracle. I was hoping for the stars to align as they can do at the Games. I was still up there with the pack, I was hoping I'd be able to break away, pull ahead, and have my last swan song.

The thing is, I wasn't the first athlete to think this and I certainly wasn't the last. You see it with athletes now, Judoka who've tried to fight their way back to the top and even if their hearts are there, their legs often aren't. It's a bit like Sebastian Coe who always seemed to have that extra gear when it mattered and then all of a sudden he didn't. Steve Ovett was the same. You have an extra gear where you can kick and win and I didn't have that, or rather I lost it somewhere along the way, and I knew it. But still, somehow I was hoping for a miracle.

I didn't get one.

That was a very strange Games. I remember we were warming up on the track in the village, doing 100m sprints and Ben Johnson was right next to us, it was like a steam train going past us, I've never seen anybody run so quick, none of us could believe it. Then later we all heard the shock and horror of the 100m and how he had tested positive. It was totally surreal. That set the tone. It was an odd Olympics. Very tense.

I went to dinner with a member of the press one night while there. I was a veteran at this point, three different Olympics and you get to know the journalists when you've been around that long. So, we chatted quite happily, over coffee, and I went back to my room ready for bed, ready to compete the next day.

The next day after competing, I went for a walk to clear my head and to get away from all the madness and disappointment. However, as I was coming into the village, the madness found me again and I got mobbed outside. Bang!

Press, cameras, television. 'Neil, what happened? Why you?' They were pointing a finger at me, I didn't know what it was all about but something had obviously leaked and something had happened. But they were pointing fingers at me! Even the journalist who I'd had coffee with me 2 nights before had a tape recorder in my face asking what was going on? I left this shower of whatever behind, went into our holding area in the village, our hostel and the whole British Judo team were there, heads down.

Kerrith Brown was on the balcony, he'd won the bronze medal but they found he had taken a diuretic to lose weight, it wasn't even a drug, not a Ben Johnson affair, but it was banned because it can be used to clear the system of other things. It was the first Olympics where it had been banned so it wasn't the worst thing, but it was against the rules and he was going to be sent home, stripped of his medal. It was a disaster. I went up to talk to him but he was just inconsolable and I can't blame the guy. I was too.

The thing that got me was that they'd pointed the finger at me, last Olympic Games, last effort, it must be him. It was either me or him, because that was the day we were competing and I thought 'why' because never, ever, ever have I gone anywhere near the line with anything like that. I was so against drug taking and anything like that which enables you to perform better. That's the thing about the diuretic, two days before, training with Kerrith, he could hardly stand up, I was half holding him up, so it hadn't helped his performance in any way, but being the athlete he was, he'd managed an amazing performance. It was one of those things that really got me thinking as to how bad the British press can be sometimes when it comes to pointing the finger without knowing all the facts and I was really disappointed with that and for Brownie.

As it was, my Games were not going to go to plan either
I had my first fight against the Portuguese and I threw him. It was a hard fight and then I had the East German in the 2nd round. This was my last Olympics, and this fight

turned out to be my last contest ever. It was hard and it was brutal, and I knew I wasn't going to win it. I knew it, and the knowing that I had that doubt was going to be my downfall. I couldn't be further from my 1981 World Champion mindset. I lost on a single small score. One that I thought was mine. My last ever fight at the Olympics, one I'd gone in to with so much stress and outside pressure and it was a fraction of a score that ended it all. Somehow, that made it worse. I stepped off the mat and that was it.

It was finished. I was finished. It was all over.

And then I started to find out the truth. I later found out the team manager had never wanted me there in the first place even if he was somewhere inside holding on to a slim hope of a medal chance with me. He stole my pass to the closing ceremony and hid it. Whether it was a subliminal demonstration of the frustration he felt, or all in fun as he later claimed, to me, it wasn't. It took three hours to get a new pass and when I found out, the ceremony was already under way. I missed my last Olympic Closings. I was left completely out in the cold by my team. That feeling stays with you. Again, unable to finish what I had started.

It's hard to accept, it's a journey and one that ends suddenly and a lot of time harshly. But even then, stepping off that mat, numb with loss, I knew something; I wasn't done. I was going to go somewhere else, redirect. I'm really difficult to stop that way. I needed a rest, I needed to gather my thoughts together but once that happened I knew I'd be okay.

I knew I had to get good at other things, I didn't realise at that stage that it was going to be commentary. I'd done some by 1988, the odd tape and some technical stuff but I had a long way to go to be proficient. I was coaching too and that was starting to go well and I was starting to learn the craft of coaching for different levels. For all the horrible pressure in France, I'd learned how to engage with a class and individuals and I knew there were skills there to be honed. So then, the question became:

***

For a long time, that looked like it would be Coventry Judo Club. They'd always supported me and they really needed better facilities. They had this building they'd been in for years. I remember doing Judo in their hall and sometimes it was so cold that there was literally ice on the mat. It was just miserable but I loved it, it was my home and where I'd started my journey.

When I went back to visit they said they thought they'd have to let the place go, it was coming to an end. I said 'I'm looking for a place to renovate as a potential business'. We talked about it and I asked them to give me a week before they sold the building.

Alison and I went to the bank, and talked about borrowing money. We came back to Coventry Judo Club and asked 'if we were interested in buying it, what would you sell it to us for?' They gave us an amount. The bank asked for a business plan and we were off.

Could it be that simple?

Neither Alison nor I had ever written a business plan before. Plus the building was just awful. It was barely functional and suddenly we found ourselves in a difficult situation. The amount of work it needed we just couldn't afford to borrow as well as start a business.

So, Coventry Judo Club called me in and said 'listen, we've got an idea you might like, you might not'. What about if we give you the club for a peppercorn rent of £1 a year and you then use the money that you borrow from the bank to renovate the club and get it going again?' They would also continue to use the dojo, the matted teaching hall, maintaining a home for Coventry Judo Club. That made a lot of sense because the only other choice was for them to sell it and then re-locate. The building was slowly falling down around them, they had to move and the best scenario was to sell the land, really.

So, that was the arrangement. That was my direction. We had a goal.

Builders came in, money being spent, back to bare brick, Judo guys stripping it down and we were on our way.

We had an eight-month period where work was being done to the club and was taking too long. In those 8 months, there was only money going out, not coming in.

We instantly had problems with the neighbours. They really didn't want the club there. I couldn't really get to grips with their way of thinking. I couldn't understand why they would want a derelict building just sitting there doing nothing instead of being used for something and being maintained. No end of antics started to happen: We had people poisoning our hedges. We had people blocking access. We had police called for excessive noise.

My favourite was one neighbour put in a complaint that a business could not possibly be there due to unsafe fire regulations. Her complaint was based on the idea that a fire truck wouldn't be able to attend any emergency, as it wouldn't fit down the drive and into the car park. Luckily, we had a member who was a fire fighter and cited this as complete nonsense. Literally, within ten minutes of him hearing this tid-bit, we had a full size fire truck in the middle of the car park with all lights and sirens blaring. Pictures were taken and sent in to the Council and that was the end of that. You could say I don't do things by halves.

I also had problems with the builders who turned out to be, what we call in the UK cowboy builders, and in the end I just kicked them off the site. They did come back trying to collect on their payment. At one stage in the 'discussion', one of the builders faced up to me, which was quite ironic when you think about it being a Judo club and I had some of my future students there helping me with the conversion. As the Judo lads stood up, he soon saw sense and backed down. I did, however, pay him for his materials and sent him on his way. Funnily enough, he didn't ask for a reference.

At one point, we were almost on our way to the scrapheap. My friend Bruce Newcombe, who trained there for... well... forever, was hammering away on this one wall. 'BOOM, BOOM, BOOM' we heard in rhythm. Bless him, he was so enthusiastic, but our smiles quickly faded to sheer shock when we realised he was taking out a supporting wall by mistake!

We all worked so hard, friends, and club mates. We had equipment brought in, we'd borrowed £50-60,000 and I have to tell you, we were in trouble right from the start, from the very beginning.

The whole idea of the club was to run it as a business. A health club business, not just for sports people, but for seriously unfit and/or overweight people, which is the way the gym ran for 12 years. This was an interesting comparison to what people expected of me, as they always seem to expect me to be teaching at high-level and coaching at an elite level.

So there were two different levels of the club. There were the health club members. It really was the 'Cheers' of the health club business as it was a small club with approximately 400 members at its peak. And then we had a full-time dojo, which catered for Judo, Karate, and a developing full-time Judo training centre for our youngsters. What I wanted and what was successful was having a full-time Judo school with the main points of the school being a skills centre in order to develop competition skills in athletes.

This worked really well over the 12-year period and meant that I had many international players of all levels coming to the centre to learn skills from me. In fact, many future World and Olympic Champions came to the club just for the skill sessions which, in turn helped my developing full-time youngsters. Many of my youngsters were aged from 13 years of age right the way through to 17-18 years of age. Obviously the 13 year olds started part-time until they finished school and then came into the centre to start Judo full time.

Full-time Judo really is all about doing preparation: physical preparation, skills preparation, and competition preparation. I know I keep knocking on about preparation but it really is the key! It is about preparing the Judoka for high-level competition and coaching, being able to pass on their skills after their competition Judo career is finished. We had much success over the 12 years, winning over 30 national senior titles, as many junior national titles, and many of the full timers being selected for European, World and Olympic Games.

We had a great program as far as international fighters using the centre as preparation for World and Olympic Games and using it as part of their preparation. Many of these fighters are now themselves great coaches and have coached Olympic and World champions themselves. This, for me, was the greatest success of the program, and was not only my education as a coach, but the education for each of the players to pass on to future generations.

Having a full-time group was a great education for me as a developing coach and it taught me how to develop programs for athletes transitioning through to international competition. I was able to develop and improve the skills base for all of the athletes that came to the club. This is why the club was internationally known as the 'go-to' skills centre.

I was also travelling internationally a lot and I realised that I needed help in order to deliver the program to the full-time students. This is where John Hennessey came in as part of the program in 1992 to help me when I couldn't be at every training session with the students. Every full-time program needs a second-in-command to help to support not only the physical side of the program but the coach administration side of things. He became a dear friend and ally throughout the years and the whole process helped him to become a great coach too. The students knew that if I wasn't there, John would be, and that made all the difference with the continuity and consistency of the program.

Of course I had my ups and downs with many of the students. Some of them I didn't feel were pulling their weight and of course there was the odd altercation with them in regards to taking soft drink stock without paying (I must still have the stack of IOUs somewhere!), a general lack of consideration for other paying club members and for Alison and I who were like second parents to a lot of the younger ones.

Lee Burbridge must hold the record for the amount of times being 'kicked out' of the programme, only to come back, head hung low asking to be forgiven for whatever stunt he had pulled that week or month. I was a tough coach, maybe too tough at some points. I made it very clear that I was not a part of their social scene and kept that line drawn very tightly. Again, probably too tight. I didn't want to become their babysitter. That is why I drew that line so tersely, but maybe I could have been more understanding, or more sensitive to their needs.

I knew what I did to become champion and thought that this is the way all athletes should go. Why not? It works, right? It didn't even occur to me that maybe that wasn't the way all people worked; that maybe different personalities needed different things to grow. I ran the programme fundamentally as: either you were fit to do it, or you weren't. If I could do it again, I would find a middle ground, which I think I found later on when working with the Belgian team.

I think looking back that most athletes who are focused and have a particular plan are self-centred and generally interested in themselves and not those around them. As are most teenagers, to be fair. So we had a double dose of it. I'm going through it yet again with my two daughters now! However, I am now very close to many of my former students. My children have played with their children growing up and I have certain business ventures with some of them. I enjoy a life-long relationship with many of them. I like to think that a lot of their foundation as human beings was laid with the help of the Judo program and the ethics that it involves. I must have done something right because I look at them now and I am so very proud of their achievements both on and off the mat!

There was one time I remember when I was really disappointed with their lack of thought, as coaches can do from time to time, and I had to go to London for a day on business afterwards. When I returned from London, all I saw was paint-covered students who had taken the whole day to paint my dojo, three times over, while I was away. Not only did it look like a professional job, but it was also testament to how they felt about the club, and me.

To say that I was choked, in a good way, is an understatement and I realised that they were all growing up into good people. Of course, it was very important for them to be good at Judo to win medals but at one stage in their lives they had to know that there were things in life other than Judo.

Other times, I was their big brother. You know the type. The older sibling who only plays games they know they are going to win or make the rules to such an end. That was me, completely. An example was King's Hill. Ask any of the full timers about King's Hill and you'll see them bend a little at the knees in recollection.

I was always playing mind games with them, throwing challenges at them and trying to motivate them in different ways. I remember one time, Lee Burbridge (again!) was complaining about doing King's Hill and that he was tired.
'We're all tired,' I said, 'but sometimes we just have to get on with it.'

So I offered a challenge. I said to the boys to select their best two runners and I will run King's Hill back to back. If one of their runners beat me on either of the laps I would pay them £5.

What they wanted to do, though, is all 3 of us go together one circuit around King's Hill, which would have meant definite defeat for me, as they were better runners. So, what I suggested to them was that we would run individual laps in pairs, for 2 circuits around for me, one with each of them, this would mean we would have to dig in and use our hearts and determination when the going got tough, depending only on our selves and our individual mentality, not depend on the 'team mate' to pace each other . I think it was Jamie Johnson first time round which I only just barely won, and then I had to leave immediately with Burbridge for the second lap. The King's Hill run was 5 miles long but particularly difficult because it was up and down hills and it was in five sections. I was training for the London Marathon at that point so it was helpful for me as well, not only to get the miles in, but to test my own grit.

Burbridge was a much better runner than me and was so confident on the way round that he was running backwards while I was running forwards. There was a straight part of the run that was, in fact, the longest part of the run and was only the fourth length.

As I rounded the corner ready to start the fifth and final length, I nearly ran over Lee, who had stopped dead at the traffic lights that marked the fifth length. There was still another mile to go. He stood there blinking as he realised that he still had the final run to the club. He had given it his all and had nothing left. I ran past turned around running backwards grinning from ear to ear.

'What's wrong Lee? Not finished yet sunshine!' I called back to him, then turned around to sprint it back to the club, winning the race and my £5.

So once again it was a matter of age and treachery overcoming youth and talent. The boys were not happy with Burbridge. The whole idea of the run was for them to realise that we all get tired but sometimes we have to dig in and overcome our fatigue.

We had lots of similar lessons throughout our 12 years some of which they carry with them and use on their own students in a similar way. They were always determined to beat me and it seemed to put an edge to our relationship. I was always playing games on them trying to be challenging and trying to motivate them in different ways.

On another occasion they challenged me, determined to get the best of me just once! The challenge was a one off, fastest runner once around King's Hill and the loser paid a forfeit. Again they wanted to go with me one-on-one, but again, I refused. I said I would take that challenge but running as individuals and the fastest time wins. They agreed with no hesitation. I should have known then they were up to something!

Being super sneaky as they were, they selected their best runner and decided that they would plant one of the boys in a car halfway around the course to drive them a part of the way. Knowing that I would smell a rat if they came in too quickly, they calculated that the car would just take the runner to just before the turning, drop them off to run in making it in a time just quicker than our best time ever recorded.

And it worked. I was baited. As I was going second, there was a very despondent me. I was facing defeat as our old record had just been beaten! However, a very determined Neil Adams decided to show them that you had to try, dig in and die on that course (or mat, really) trying.

I decided to go out as quickly as possible and push through the second part of the course, hoping not to completely die. The Universe was on my side that day as somehow I managed to dig in on that second half of the course and beat their time by 10 seconds. It didn't matter how much they checked their watches, I had beaten their time! I smiled smugly as I held out my hand and claimed my forfeit.

It didn't stop with running and it was all about the next challenge, and the challenge after that. The next challenge being a weights-based challenge. After carefully assessing their chances, gauging the weights exercises they were good at versus the ones I was good at, they came up with a mixture of exercises, incorporating muscular endurance linked to weight or power.

There were several exercises as part of the challenge and again, as the challenges were meant to do, pushed them to do better than normal or better than what they thought they could achieve. It's because of this that it was all evens and they look set to win on the last exercise.

This last exercise was Dave Nichols' favourite: the fly press. He was better than anybody in the club. The boys were already relishing the victory, and started to celebrate… just a little bit too early though. Dave decided to go for the big weight immediately so as to start the celebrations in earnest. On to the machine he jumped, confident in his prowess and locked in on the fly bars. He pushed, and he pushed, his face changing colour and contorting to an expression of desperation! He failed the weight!! He went too high a weight too early, thinking he would get it over and done with. This meant that I only had to do a 5kg push to win yet another challenge. I won't say they hated me but they didn't like me very much at the time. There were times when they did have success but this is my book after all.

The challenges never stopped and the lessons learnt were life lessons.

Of course the full-time training at the club was my interest as a coach, but Alison and I realised we had to make the business work as well. To say that we were naïve in business is an understatement, certainly me much more than Alison, and on reflection we should've done advance sales on the membership site to help pay for our bank loan.

We had borrowed a lot of money to renovate the building and when I look back we were always going to have a problem paying it off. It was all about how many members we could get in to the club, how many we could retain on an annual basis, and whether we could pay the monthly bills.

At the beginning it was very slow and looking back we were lucky to have a very understanding bank. That is until 1990 when the interest rates spiked. Suddenly, our loan that we were already struggling to pay back became impossible.

It already was a constant battle to make ends meet and to pay the bills. We were charging tuition for the full-time training, however a lot of parents were finding it difficult to pay and we went sometimes months without that money coming in. In fact, at times it was only the memberships for the club that was keeping us afloat. The difference, and maybe our saving grace between us and the larger clubs, was that we offered personalised attention with the members of the club and gave them a personal direction. It was all about retention. It was the only way we could survive. If we lost a member to the big clubs, there was very little we could offer to get them back other than personal time and effort for each member, which really was unsustainable.

When we moved from London to the Midlands, we elected to move near Mum & Dad in Wellesbourne, near Stratford-upon-Avon. As chance would have it a house came up in their area and it was a short commute to the club. It was also a help to have Mum & Dad close by for those times we needed childcare, however this didn't happen a lot of the time as Ashley had started attending the Croft School in nearby Stratford-upon-Avon.

You'll hear people still talk about 1990, when the banks raised their interest rates. The banks found their managers had been too liberal with lending money and now found themselves in a right state. The management level was sacked, the interest rates were spiked, and many, many businesses went pop.

We were also in this line of fire and our monthly payments went through the roof. We really had to sit down and look at where we were at in terms of feasibility and question as to whether we could we keep the club running. I called in a favour with a friend, the Chairman of the Budokwai Club then, Brian Davis. He was much more knowledgeable dealing with banks then I ever was. He helped us immensely. I remember going into the bank meeting and him telling them that they would do better to wipe some of the debt away to let us to continue to trade, than to have us go bankrupt and the bank lose all their money. That, as well as being tied to a building of no real value due to its position and zoning. I walked out of that meeting having agreed to downsize my house to pay back some of the loan, but also in complete bewilderment of how a sizeable chunk of the loan was just whisked away. I didn't really understand it all or how it happened, but was glad of all it really. The For Sale sign went up in Wellesbourne, and one came down on Green Lane, Coventry, directly across from the club which we were able to buy with a bit of released equity from the sale and nestled in amongst the neighbours who, ironically, had given us such trouble in the past.

So, from the outside, the building looked beautiful and the club looked as if it was thriving. Inside, like other things, it was not so pretty.

***

Alison and I by this time had been through so much stress with the business and that wasn't helping our marriage, which was also, again, under a lot of stress. I think the both of us were concentrating on the wrong things, trying to make the business work more than our family life. In the end, looking back, I think Alison could see that the club was dying, as was our marriage, before I did. I think as far as I was concerned, I was trying to keep myself busy, which wasn't difficult, as I was travelling such a lot and concentrating on the full-time students and of course, Ashley.

It was around the mid '90s that Alison decided that she needed to be independent from not only me, but also that she needed independence in case we were to split. Probably the whole bank thing shook her up more than I thought, and I was travelling a lot with the GB Team preparing for the

'96 Olympics Games in Atlanta, so I suspect this started her thinking of what would be her Plan B, if needed.

The club was certainly dying, so Alison concentrated on a sports science degree and put all of her time into it. This meant that I spent a lot of time alone with Ashley and inevitably drifted further and further away from Alison, however, in turn creating a super strong relationship with my son.

We did manage to buy a house in Canley, Coventry. It was luck really. I had heard from a member that an old, derelict property was going up for auction, just down the road from the club. I went to look at it and decided then and there it was where our fortunes were going to take a turn for the better. That is if I could get it for a bargain.

It was sealed bids and I called the estate agent to get an idea of a guide price and what the interest was. I was told 'off the record' that there was another interested party at £80,000. I felt they were bluffing.

I put in a cheeky bid of £70,000.

On the day of the auction, the call came through that we were successful! This old farmhouse was going to be a real project, but one that we could sink our teeth into. My dad and mum had recently moved down to Devon but my dad was having trouble finding work, being new to the area. I said I would pay him to help me with this new house, so he came up to us for weeks at a time to help me with the renovations again. He is a master carpenter and made all the windows and interiors. He helped me with adding the damp course and the cleaning out the cellar and all the sandblasting. We had to remove a tree from inside at one point!

What was interesting about this house and why it was still standing, is that it made it through the Second World War bombing of Coventry. It was found in documents later that the Luftwaffe had used the farmhouse as a marker to bomb the car factories that were making the ammunitions for

WW2.

I liked the fact that the house already had a 'personality' or that it was a 'survivor'. It appealed to my nature, our need to create some equity, if not to my need for something to take my mind off of my other troubles. My thirties were ending. I needed some sort of stability.

Neil training for the Marathon

8. Hips Don't Lie

I've always loved running. It seems though that running didn't like me very much. That didn't stop me though. I ran. I ran a lot. Ok maybe not Forest Gump kind of mileage but it felt at times.

The amount of running that I did was not only from my training, but as a means of transport.

I ran to get to training.

I ran to get to work.

I ran everywhere and anywhere else I needed to be. I dare say it would have been better to have had a bike, especially when I was in London at 16 years of age, with no money and only Tube and buses to get me to destinations. A bike would have saved me a lot of pounding of the pavements to get to places. The way I looked at it, at the time, was that it served two purposes: one - to get me there, and another to lay my cardio foundation.

When I look at runners now I see how easy it is to become obsessed with running. Many runners that I see seem to be almost fanatical with it to the degree that it can be unhealthy on the body and the mind. It is amazing how many will still run even though they're injured. This is exactly what happened to me. I became obsessed with the importance of running to improve my fitness for Judo training. Of course there is no substitute for Judo itself and no amount of running can prepare you for the needs of Judo.

I suppose you could say that I was hooked, a runoholic, and preferred to run as opposed to other cardiovascular exercises that I could have been doing and that would've been much better in the long run on my body. The accumulation of constant pounding was to have a profound effect on my hips and my knees in later years and instead of being a stress release, it just added to the stress my body was enduring through over training.

Why was I so obsessed with running is the question?

One of the main reasons for me was there it was one of the most difficult stand-alone cardiovascular training that you could ever do. If you cycle, row, cross train or whatever form of cardiovascular training you decide to do, if you get tired you can always back-track, ease off the pedal and release the pressure. With running you are out there on your own with nobody to help you and often with no other way to get back home other than your own two legs. I think this is what the appeal was. It was dig in, it was individual, and you can do it anywhere at any time. Oh yeah, and it didn't cost me a thing… well in pound coins anyways.

The strange thing was that for a reasonably muscular Judo body weighing approximately 80 kg I was surprisingly quite quick. Of course I wasn't the right shape or body make up for really fast speeds but I was definitely persistent and I was able to grind out some reasonable times. My 10 KM times were always around about 40 minutes, although I have to say that I never broke the 40 minute mark. It was always approximately 20 seconds over the 40 minutes. This was me, always trying to better myself trying to achieve something, trying to better myself every time I ran.

It was back in the early 1990's that Ezio Gamba, my opponent in the 1980 Olympic final and who won the split decision, mentioned to me about running the London Marathon. In a phone call, he mentioned that he had always wanted to run a marathon and he suggested maybe we could run it together.

This is one of the most incredible things of our sport, that many of the fighters who I have fought in major competition, not only have become good friends but we also have the privilege of doing crazy things together many years after we have competed together on the greatest stage of all. We all remain good friends and create friendships that will last a lifetime.

Having run within Ezio on numerous occasions and ascertaining from this that I was probably a little bit faster than Ezio, I realised that our preparation and pace for the marathon would probably be a little different. The fact that we were training in two different countries meant that we could train at our own pace. I don't know if that was good or bad, really.

Of course, I realised that this distance was all about preparation, and the distance of 26 miles needed to be treated with the utmost respect. You need to put your miles in, I was told, and you have to make sure that you get the pace right when you run it. This is all great advice but it seemed to go out of the window not only when preparing for the marathon, but when I was eventually to run it a couple of years later.

We started to put the miles in, me in the UK and Ezio, in Italy. We talked often on the phone about our preparation, about how difficult it was and of course about our aches and pains. But we both thought that as we were two very determined fighters, this would help us to dig in and to succeed in the end.

I was using anyone at the club who wanted to go for a run as a training partner for my daily runs. If I was obsessed before, this certainly intensified it tenfold. Now I was a fanatic, so that meant everybody at the club had to be too. Alison was also running it, however, elected to do her own training and very few times did we do a training run together. It was always a competition to me, and not so much for her, so it didn't suit either of us, as her way wasn't enjoyable for me; there was no real goal other than doing the mileage. I couldn't have been much fun for her, either, as I was pushing, pushing, pushing, all the time, living on the edge of pain. As I started to increase my mileage and running twice a day instead of only once, I did start to get tired and worn, but would run through the pain because in my mind, I had a goal and I was determined to reach it.

It was not a normal goal either. It was one that I had in my mind and it was an achievement above the norm. Every Judo player that I spoken to prior to the marathon had run approximately anywhere between 3h 30m to the 4 hour mark, and they were happy that this was a respectable time, especially for a Judoka.

I didn't just want to beat this time I wanted to *obliterate* it.

I had a set in my mind to run a sub 3 hour marathon and Ezio had 3 hours 30 as his benchmark and Alison a sub 4 hours.

We started to build up the miles (or km in Ezio's case) and I never thought that I would ever refer to 10 miles as a short run. Some of the runs were now starting to build up to 15 miles and I was starting to approach the 20 mile mark.

I remember this one time about 13 miles into the run I

was running through a little village and had absolutely nothing left in the tank. This was the run that made me realise that water alone was not enough, and that I would need electrolyte fluids from now on if I was going to make it to the end.

I saw a phone box in the village that I was passing through. I stumbled over to it and then fell into it to call the club.

'Please, could someone come and collect me?' I heaved out in between breaths.

I didn't even have the strength to step outside the phone box and was still there, in the exact same position 30 minutes later when they arrived. I hadn't moved an inch.

On another occasion I remember the full-time trainers saying to me how tired they were for randori practice and how they wanted to rest. So I said to them, 'I will do my 15 mile run during the day and then randori in the evening.' For those of you that don't know what randori practice is? It is our form of free fighting that requires movement, technique, explosiveness and stamina. It is our form of free fighting or sparring.

After falling through the door at the club after 15 miles and being aware that I had to keep true to my word, I slipped on my Judogi in the reception area where I had fallen, ready for my evening's practice. I believe it was the only time in my history of Judo that I have practiced with another person without moving my feet in any way whatsoever. They were rooted to the floor. My mind was willing but my body was not. My legs revolted, my feet were on strike. However, it made a point, and at least the boys didn't complain about being tired again. I think they felt sorry for me and helped me stand up the entire practice.

One of my biggest mistakes in training for this marathon was that I didn't do enough miles and I was to pay the price, big time, come race day.

Ezio and I started the race together with a plan in our heads and each with an objective. The atmosphere on the start line was of a street party rather than a marathon. There were thousands of runners, fun runners, serious runners, people dressed in many incredible costumes running for their different charities and I remember starting the race with a smile on my face and full of expectation.

Little was I to know that the smile would be categorically wiped off my face and how I would suffer later on.

I passed through the half marathon in less than 1 ½ hours and I thought that everything was going according to plan. But when I got to about 17 miles I hit that dreaded wall. It wasn't a bump. It wasn't a bang. It was a BAAM!

I've heard so many stories of people hitting the wall and really, I didn't know what it meant. I think it was at this moment that I realised that I should've done the high mileage, over 20 miles, in practice at least once. Great advice given to me after!

They say hindsight is a great thing but looking back I see that this contributed to me not having anything left at 17 miles and still having 9 miles to go. My other major mistake was not pacing myself correctly. I got carried away with the carnival atmosphere of the run. I thought 'well, I can't be in the same group as Batman and Big Bird! I'm an elite athlete!'

I knew I was in trouble when Batman, Big Bird and Mickey Mouse came jogging passed me at mile 17. I was really going to have to pull out all the resources in order to finish. That, or use the rest of my energy to batter someone in costume to steal it and disguise myself.

I can honestly say I have never felt more like stopping in my whole life. I eventually got to the bridge and the finishing line was just across the other side. I remember putting one foot and then the second foot over the line and stopping. Of course there are many people coming over the line at same time and one of the controllers tried to hurry me along. I turned on him with a look of pure hatred and threatened him with his life if he didn't take his hands off of me. He, then, quite wisely, backed away and left me alone.

Somehow I had lost 40 minutes in the last 7 miles and eventually came in with 3 hours 44 mins. Alison was only 4 minutes behind me and said to me afterwards,

'If I had known I was so close to you I would have sped up!'

I said, 'I would have rugby tackled you first'.

And she knew I meant it. Not to say she didn't do an amazing time in her first marathon. She did.

Was I happy with my run? I was devastated. I felt that I had failed. To make things worse Ezio came in at just over 3 hours and 30 minutes but that was typical Ezio, tactical and efficient.

After the marathon I vowed never to run a marathon again, it cured me of my 'addiction' then and there. It did make me look at the mileage that I was doing for training and it made me realise that a lot of my injuries were probably through excessive, high-impact exercise, and I looked carefully at other alternatives as well as the running. I had to look for a balance.

Jumping quickly forward, to my 40s, I knew that my knees and my hips were in particular bad condition. My knees have been able to carry on just as 'post competitive injuries'. My hips on the other hand, were a different story. My back would seize up. I couldn't stand for longer than 10 minutes without the pain shooting down my groin. It took me 15 minutes each morning to get out of bed and like an old car, warm up into moments to start off each day. I've heard a lot of stories of runners who after excessive mileage have had really bad injuries in later life and have had to stop running altogether. I was in this group suddenly, and painfully.

Doctor after doctor kept X-Raying me for my back until one doctor finally said, 'have you had your hips checked?'

My hips? I haven't done anything to my hips, but hey, I was willing to go with anything at this point. And there it was: hip sockets showing bone on bone, grinding against each other. No wonder my back was screaming at me. There was no cushion there at all. And my knees? Really an over compensation for what was happening above them.

Luckily in 2006, a very dear friend, Terry Welham in Cambridge, a former Police Detective who sadly is no longer with us, knew the specialist there. I had taught for him in Cambridge for many years and was able to get in quite quickly once the problem had been revealed. This doctor was one of the 'disciples' of the Birmingham Hip group who had first pioneered the procedure and was somewhat disturbingly keen to get me under the knife. As the gas was administered, and I was going under, he looked me straight in the eye and said, 'I think I'll be the only one in history that can say, I knocked Neil Adams unconscious!' His smiling face blurred away into the blackness.

So I came out of that operation as part Titanium Man. Niki offered but I refused to wear a cape. The pain was gone and replaced by a new pain: airport security. I buzz every time I walk through and that's a lot with 26 different events to go commentate every year.

The hip operation was the best thing I could have ever done for myself. I am a new man! The doc then did say the other would have to be done as well but I had a few years yet. I really concentrated on my pre-habilitation, which I really believe was the key to success. The doctor told me he had himself and two assistants heaving on my leg to dislocate it so as to get in to work on the socket, so I'm happy to say they had a bit of a work out as well. It also tells me that I did it correctly, as the muscles were well formed and ready to heal quickly after the operation.

As you have read in *A Life In Judo*, I'm always very keen to get back into fighting fitness and this was no exception. I was told to rest for 2 weeks, but I knew I could do a little bit here and there to keep the old ticker going. Niki was having none of it.

As I relied on her the first 2-3 weeks to get me in and out of bed, she took full advantage and curtailed any ideas I had on starting my rehabilitation regime, immediately. I was literally under house arrest. I must have been a right pain in the ass as she finally cracked and brought me some dumbbells over from our gym so I could do some upper body exercises.

After my enforced rest of 2 weeks, Niki, my warden, lifted the restrictions on the gym and helped me across the courtyard to my man cave. I couldn't quite sit the bike yet, nor did they want me to, but I managed to get on the C2 rowing machine. I placed an exercise mat on the floor and took my trainer off, leaving my sock on. This allowed for my foot to slide along while my 'good' leg bent and pushed along with the upper body rowing. It was a 3-limbed row and I was sorted. Little by little, I would pull in my leg to bend the knee and flex the hip each time I did a row, which was every day, so this work perfectly. I was back on the mat demonstrating within 6 months and doing some randori within 9 months.

Three years later, in 2009 I had the other hip done and this time it was ceramic. It doesn't feel any different from the titanium one other than it doesn't vibrate when I pass under electrical wires or go near mobile tower masts. I don't do as much randori as I would like anymore as my range has been affected a bit. Those who know my technique can tell the range of my favourite throw, Tai Otoshi has lessened slightly, but I can deal with that. Most people can't tell I've had both hips done, so for that me, that's a win.

What would I tell my younger self in terms of running and

training? I would definitely do things differently and search out the many forms of cardiovascular training with focus on low impact and less chances of injury. To be honest, it's only Judo practice that is ever going to give you the cardio fitness you need for the job, so concentrate on that, I would advise. If you're going to 'run', chase the randori practices. Find as many Judo clubs and BJJ clubs as you can and get your cardio there. Your body will thank you later on.

Saying that, I do admit I miss running, but I definitely don't miss the pain.

The '96 Olympic Coaching Team calling from the sidelines

9. The '96 Disaster

In 1996, I was back at the Olympics, this time as the coach for Great Britain. I was coaching now at the very highest level leading the British team. I was making decisions that some people liked and some people really didn't. Management got a little bit hairy with the decisions I tried to make because it wasn't what they quite expected. But I took chances and I was doing it my way. I wanted to live and die by my own sword, as it were.

A coach doesn't just supervise training and advise their fighters, you have the final cut on the team and weight class assignment. I had one of my full time students who ended up not going, although I could have sent him, and it would have most likely been accepted. But it had to be a choice made for success with as little risk as possible. I had learned that from my own 1980 decision. I put one of the male fighters, who was a European Champion in his particular weight, up a weight class because the junior who was coming through was, I thought, a potential world beater and did become World champion in that weight two years later. So I did take chances on things. But they were calculated risks, with a bit of intuition thrown in. I tried to do it my way but certain members of the establishment were not always happy with it. The feeling was so fraught with uncertainty, the team selection responsibility as well as the training plan was taken off me and a selection committee was formed. Crazy really, because if they wanted a scapegoat if things went wrong, it would have totally been on my head and not the Committee's. As it was, it didn't matter anyway.

As we were coming up to the Olympics, it was the first time we had to qualify people under an international qualification system. So each of the athletes couldn't just be the best in Britain and represent Britain to be there. They had to qualify through European and World rankings by accumulating points from different events. That was both difficult and new. I had to get my head wrapped around how we could best get points and still train my athletes for the event without burning them out.

It was difficult. It was also the first time it had ever been done. We'd always sent teams to the Olympic Games well rested, well prepared and just the best in the country but this was different.

Potentially we had an amazing team. On paper, we had nine World and European medallists in the team. There was an overall expectation for medals at the Olympic Games, looking for our first Gold and we were confident. However, when we got there it all went wrong, so terribly pear shaped. All of the athletes were physically and mentally tired. They were beat, both metaphorically and literally, before we got to Atlanta and many performed below expectation. I think 8 of them were probably in the position I was in '88 where they'd decided they wanted just one more event, it was their swan song. They were part of this big group that were at the

Olympic Games to be at the Olympic Games, not necessarily to get the medal. I'd felt that pull myself so I sympathise to some degree with how it was.

I did the best I could to get them all ready. But that new process was just brutal and I was focused on getting a full team to Atlanta. To do this I had to put them in too many events to get their points. Looking back now, I would probably have taken the athletes who had the stamina to last, who wanted the medal, not the experience and I would have spaced it out a lot differently. Knowing what I know now is that one of the biggest problems athletes have, at the moment, is preparation in between events.

At some events, fighters are chasing qualification points but the problem with travelling from competition to competition is that you're not prepared properly and then you don't get past the 1st or 2nd round of the event. You need to know what period of time you've got to prepare for each event. Running and physical training is not enough, you need sparring partners too. Like I say, 90% of those chasing points are going from event to event, but not actually able to properly prepare for them.

Presently, the top fighters that have high World ranking points accumulated early are able to choose their events more carefully in their run up to the big events such as Grand Slams, World Championships & Olympic Games. They will choose the high point scoring events and prepare for 8 or 10 weeks leading up to those events.

That system in '96 was very demanding and it was not my only problem. As certain selections were taken away from me prior to the Games by the selection panel, the Olympic team that went out there was not my Olympic selection. The incredible thing was that when it all went belly up, the management left as soon as a flight could carry them back to the UK, which left me in the Olympic village alone to deal with the Press. All of the team disappeared, as did all of the management and support. They left me to carry the can. The

Press was pointing the finger at me yet again. Something I just can't forget.

Coming back from '96, British Judo moved me sideways. No surprise really as all team managers/coaches in the past were made redundant. It is an occupational hazard in British Judo. I was told they still wanted me involved but they were going to try something else. I was made a technical advisor, which basically meant I was fired, just not straight away. Knowing this and thinking this is what the whole of the UK must be feeling just destroyed me.

I was so angry with the way British Judo was treating me. The fact my team selection had been hobbled just before the Games made it even worse. Why wasn't I given the chance to run the team the way I was told I'd be allowed? I'd have gone in there, done my best and if it hadn't worked I'd have been fired and for good reason.

You see it every season with football now but somehow Judo still isn't there. I wasn't the first one they did it to and I certainly will not be the last. In reality, Olympic Team Mangers need to be given a 4 or an 8 year cycle and given a chance to see it through.

I was hung out to dry to take the blame from the athletes, the Federation, the Press and all of the UK, who all had high expectations for these Games, and that has stuck with me. I found the hard way just how fickle people can be.

I was the Golden Boy of British Judo as a competitor. Once my job of winning medals was done though, the sparkle and shine soon left. When I started to come into the coaching sphere, it was definitely BJA Chairman, George Kerr at the time, that wanted me in there as the head coach. I think that was a mistake, although I appreciated his faith in me.

Even today, as it should have been then, what needs to happen is the creation of a two tier coaching system.

Certainly, coaching is a young man's game when it's day to day with the athlete. That was where my skills lay. There's a lot of different types of coaches but I was great with individuals and rock solid on skills. That's my approach to this day and when left to do it, I can really make a difference in someone's overall game and skill base. But being left to do it all alone, like I was, it wasn't enough. I needed a bit of shelter. There needs to be a council of elders too. The veteran coaches looking in from above, protecting the coaches and the athletes, correcting junior coaches when needed and protecting them when they have to. I needed that. I really needed a trustworthy, experienced elder statesperson or mentor to bounce ideas off of, not a selection committee made up of paper pushers and people pleasers. There was no coaching pathway, I went from competitor to Head Coach in quick succession with only my wits about me. I did what I thought was right at the time, and did the best with what I had. What I didn't have was that sword to live or die by. I was led like a goat to slaughter, however.

I was on one ALMIGHTY low when I came back from that Olympic Games and some, if not all, to some degree, of the athletes blamed me for the team's failure. I could understand why but some of the decisions I took the blame for were not mine. Some decisions were, of course, and I stand by them. I used to put players back to back fighting each other if I had more than one in a weight category and that got some people's hair up. But it kept them motivated, and on their toes, knowing whoever got the best score was going to come out ahead. It was a tough choice but competing at this level you have to fight for your spot. You can't be trapped in the pack.

So they didn't like that and they also didn't like being moved up and down through weight classes. However, those were my decisions and I stand by them. I'm really sorry for how things went but, to their credit, the athletes who did blame me are now coaches themselves and now see with what I had to do and deal. Some have apologised personally to me about their behaviour in the past, now knowing how it all works and so have I. The fact is, you don't know what you don't know.

During the process, at one of the training camps, one athlete did call me out though. I had put him up a category and brought the junior up into his weight. He got drunk one night, stood in the middle of the hotel courtyard, yelling up at my balcony and called me out. I knew if I'd gone out there, let him take a swing at me, it would have cost him the Olympic place. Looking back now, I probably should have fronted it. I didn't at the time because I didn't want it to cost him his Olympic place, something that was his life's passion. I didn't want him to lose that over one stupid, drunken decision. On reflection I should have been tougher. My respect for him and his dreams outweighed my need for respect from the team as I believe they all saw my non-responsiveness to his challenge as cowardice. Answering him, going out there for 'a duel' may have been the cement I needed to create the team atmosphere, support and cohesiveness I so greatly needed going into the Games. But I was not there to be their friends. I was there to be the coach and leader and paid to make the tough decisions. I guess I should have let him have his chance at me. It most likely wouldn't have changed the outcome in any case.

Those Olympics were a disaster for British Judo and it was for me as well. Not just because of the failure of the team but because I was trying to establish myself as a coach and a world class coach at that. For that to not work, and also not be Olympic champion? The cloud just seemed to be getting darker and darker.

However, they were lessons and I learned them. The hard way. Because in the end that's all you can do. I knew they were going to eventually get rid of me, so, again, I started thinking about what was next.

10. Ending and Beginning

They say a rut is a shallow grave. That's where I was and I spent the rest of 1996 trying to get out of it.

That started with the club. I redirected my energies into the full time training group and making the club work. It was nowhere near as satisfying as being a competitor and nowhere near as satisfying as being national coach and winning Olympic medals and stuff like that, at least at first. The come down from competing at the highest level is huge and I felt it every day.

Judo, at last, was starting to be a calm place in my life. My marriage, on the hand, was not.

In 1998 I turned 40. What did I want at 40 years old? We all assess or re-assess our lives at 40 but not until we have a bit of a celebration. Alison and my family surprised me at her father's restaurant near Oxford with all the old Judo fraternity showing up. I was genuinely surprised as it was made out it was just going to be a family dinner. It was a total surprise when I walked into the restaurant to find so many of my Judo colleagues, friends, and family there for my surprise party. It was a great time and I enjoyed seeing everyone again. It was great to know that people still thought of me enough to make the time and effort to be there. It was also a bit sad, as I knew I wasn't happy and I knew Alison wasn't happy either. The worse thing was I didn't know what to do about it all. Becoming 40 really was a time for me to take a real, hard look at my life. I found myself saying more and more often, 'Is this it?'

The thing was that Alison and I were spending so much time away from each other, I guess we were also both reassessing our futures. We were both struggling with our relationship and looking for something else. Looking back to this time I realised that at this stage I was starting to drink too much and it was very much affecting the way I was and certainly not helping me in sorting out my problems. I think that many people when they start to drink too much have a reason for doing it, and I think in my case it was a mixture of many things. It was much easier to deal with everything in a fuzz or a numbed-out state. Rather than solving the problem, drinking too much created more heartache and problems.

Alison and I had both realised there was something drastically wrong with the relationship. She tried to address my drinking, dealing with it head on, with a no-nonsense attitude and that only caused more conflict. After denial comes defence, but it's all fodder for arguments. By this stage it was really starting to upset Ashley too. He loved me unequivocally but when I had a drink, he didn't like me. He had reason to. I wasn't a nice person when I'd had a drink, I was not happy. I was never abusive, maybe verbally so, but I never lashed out. I was very defensive if any one tried to point it out and said I should get help. I was super fit, trained every day, never missed work, so 'what are they on about?' was my attitude towards it all.

Niki put it in perspective years later that although I wasn't abusive, I wasn't *there*. That was it, I would just zone out, sit there in a haze and would only speak out if anyone tried to get through to me or try to disturb that blissful fuzziness of thoughtlessness. And that's what it was really, thoughtlessness, as I was not thinking of the ramifications to those around me and how much pain I was causing them. Niki said to me once, which did start the process that she wanted a partner, someone sharp to help her with business decisions and with the family and to be *present*, to be *there*.

With me, it was something that crept up on me and I didn't realise how it was affecting the people closest to me. I thought it was only affecting me, and even then I was still training and functioning as normal, or so I thought. It was a really difficult time for me as I was close to Alison's family too. When we did eventually split up I felt that they, as well as Ashley, blamed me for the split and this meant that I sadly lost contact with them along with the closeness with Ashley. I can't really blame them, as I was the one to leave. However, it was futile to stay. We would have just continued to hurt each other and for what reason? Just so as not to say, it didn't work out? To admit that we were no longer happy?

It wasn't a great model for Ashley either, and I wanted him to know what a happy relationship looks like and feels like. Everyone deserves happiness and it has taken me a very long time, and probably still not quite there, to not totally blame myself for what happened. I do have Ashley as a result of that relationship and I wouldn't trade that, and I have a friend, in Alison. We probably get along better now than ever, and I'm really glad about that, if not for our sakes, for Ashley's.

My marriage to Alison by the late 1990s was at an end and I don't know if the millennium had anything to do with it, the idea of all things changing and all things new in a new century, but in 2000, before I went to commentate at the Sydney Olympic Games we decided to call time on our marriage.

It was only sadness really.

I don't know if that it was feeling like we failed at something, or the fact that maybe we really didn't focus on what was wrong and try to make it right. Or maybe sad because we always really knew that we couldn't make it right and that we were never really meant to be partners that way. That maybe, we were always just meant to be good friends.

There was no real screaming or carrying on. Only the kind that comes from hurt and not understanding what is going on, or trying to find blame for something that didn't work. I think we just both knew it was done. It had turned into a brother and sister relationship and I will always wish happiness for Alison and do care what happens to her. I wish her well, as a brother would, and am glad in the fact she has met someone decent and good in Lloyd, her new husband. Indeed, I think they are much more compatible in their natures, than she and I would ever have been.

So, why did I drink?

I think it was to mask some of the failures, especially in the marriage. We were in this awful, complicated space where we were more friends than absolutely in love with one another and realising that, facing it, and trying not to hurt our son in the process took a very long time. Funny how the act of trying not to hurt someone's feeling in turn, hurts them even more in the end.

That's a difficult realisation to come to terms with because it feels like failure. It's not though. However, there is a grieving process that one needs to go through. You think of it as a loss but more in the form of failure than you do of something that is no longer there, at least in our case, I believe.

There's huge expectation on, and from, you both to find something ideal in the relationship. My parents have it, they've now been married for 63 years, they've been together for 70 years and my dad just dotes on my mother. I always wanted that, I always felt that that would be perfect to have that.

I haven't got a bad thing to say about Alison and our time together, but in all honesty we were more like brother and sister. It wasn't a physical relationship and we had been under so much stress for so long, almost from the beginning in fact, that in the end, I guess it just fell apart.

This is when my drinking too much really came to light. It was now becoming a problem but it was to get worse before it got better. For right or wrong, the reason I think we tried to make it work was because of Ashley. I love my son. Ashley is the best son anybody could have and we still have an amazing relationship but this was a horrible time for him in so many ways. He doesn't drink, and I know that part of my life is a big reason. I wish, dearly, I had addressed it then, or at least sooner than I did.

Thinking back I just wanted to bury my head. And the truth is we didn't talk about it, mainly because I did not want to talk about it. And being the sort of person I am, I knew that and wasn't able to admit it for a long time.

Now, years later, I'm so glad to say Alison and I are friends and this is great, especially for Ashley's sake but at the time it was a sad time for both of us. The collapse of our marriage, and the drinking, just danced around each other. I knew it was down to me and that it was getting progressively worse. The club was what started bringing it to a head.

At that particular time Alison and I were trying like mad but we were both naïve. The business wasn't doing well and bigger clubs were opening up fitness chains around us and they had so much more equipment than us and we couldn't hope to compete with them. So the health club side of the business was not running well. I was there from 7 in the morning to 10 at night and it got to the stage where I thought, 'is this it? Is this worth it?' We were working for nothing really. To make matters even worse, the full time trainers were coming up to retirement age and were all thinking of moving on themselves.

Then there was the money. It would have cost £200k to replace all the equipment and it would still only be a percentage of equipment of what they had at the bigger clubs. I couldn't compete with that, so another decision had to be made. Do we keep going with the club? Try to revive it? These questions brought up the same ones in a much more deeply personal area of our lives. Looking at our marriage, we realised it was beyond repair.

I was so afraid of how Ashley was going to react to all of it but I thought, this isn't helping anybody. If I'm going to go forward I've got to cut things loose. I've got to do something, find something that made me feel happy, to find fulfilment again. I can't just stay here in this situation and be as unhappy as I was, making everyone around me unhappy in the process. On reflection we were both dreadfully unhappy and we should have faced it earlier than we did. Neither one of us wanted to admit failure, and to be fair, we weren't at each other throats like you hear of other couples calling it quits, but then again, that would have meant there was something more than just acceptance of each other. Neither of us wanted to hurt Ashley either. We both are fiercely protective of him, and again, sometimes to a hindrance. Sober, I hope I was a good role model for him as a dad. This wasn't the model I wanted to show him as a husband. I had to change it, even if it meant heartache for all of us in the short term. I had to figure myself out.

It was at this time I was then getting into the commentating and journalistic side of things and I had a chance of being a commentator for the BBC at the Olympic Games in Sydney. I was also getting more work for Fighting Films, a Judo exclusive film production company based in Bristol, and I had a sense of momentum for the first time in a while. I'd been doing commentary for a long time and wanted to take it further, I wanted to get better at it. This, I thought, was a direction I could go, so I went for it.

Of course I didn't realise it was just as competitive as Judo. There's people in broadcasting that will cut your throat to commentate at the high profile events. You can be 'kindly' murdered. You've got to watch your back!

So once again, another period of my life was coming to an end and this time there was a lot to take into consideration. Alison and I started having discussions probably 12 months before the Olympics about folding the club and also splitting up.

That is such a hard knot to untie, especially when you have a child. I think that with any relationship that is floundering, you want to try to make it work and you think, well if we can instil some spark there, we'll give it a go. But it had gone too far and of course deep down we knew that.

I think I called time on the relationship. In all honesty,

I can't remember in all the commotion. At that point I was actually living in a different part of the house, a lovely, gorgeous house. Ironically, we were where we wanted to be finally, financially speaking. We both had jobs outside the club because Alison had finished her degree and found work as a Prison Governor at this point. We had this amazing house, we were financially stable and it was the end of the relationship. Such an odd and sad time.

I've rarely been sadder than when I got on the plane to the Olympics in 2000. I was desperately worried about my relationship with my son, at the end of my marriage and how Alison and I were going to part as amicably as possible. And, again, here I was, off to the Olympics. The site of so much pain and so many important events in my life.

What I didn't know was that the most important event in my life was about to happen; meeting Niki Jenkins. Not for the first time, but for the first time that mattered.

Neil with Niki

11. Niki

We'd met before, in 1993. I was Mr Adams to her because she is 15 years younger and I was the coach of the British team. She was always so respectful.

That's changed.

A little while ago I asked 'Why isn't it Mr Adams anymore?' and you know what she said? 'Oh that changed the morning after, Darling.'

There have been a few mythical stories out there of how it happened. I'm here to set the story straight. Here's how it happened: we were two booths away from each other commentating. Niki was commentating for CBC (Canadian Broadcast Company) and I was commentating for the BBC and, well, I noticed her. A lot. And often. She wore these red leather trousers which either helped the cause or didn't.

She was sat in her booth, which was situated just above the stand stairs leading to underneath the stands. I must have tried climbing those stairs a thousand times to get her attention and when I finally did, I waved and gave her my best sexy-not-too-sexy-boyish grin. She smiled, waved back but then turned her attention back to the mats. I sighed, dutifully took my seat but I couldn't help myself, my attention kept being drawn over to where she was sitting, which wasn't easy as there was a very rotund man from French Canadian TV sitting between us. Then all of sudden, she turned to me, looked at me straight with one of those 'hell bent' looks she is now known for, and got up from her chair and strode over to me. The first thing she said was; 'Hello Mr Adams. I was hoping I could get an interview?' She was there as part of the TEAM Toronto 2008 Task Force that was sent over bidding for the 2008 Olympics. So she wanted me to do an interview for them. She was on an information-gathering mission about how the Judo event was run; what worked and what didn't. We were together for 5 days and that spark was instantaneous. It was an immediate bond that I'm happy to say, grows every single day.

I was completely honest too. I said that I was splitting up with my wife and of course she was a bit reserved about that as she had just split up from a complicated relationship herself. 'Yes sure, I get it.' I don't think she did, as she was pretty surprised when I called her on the way back from Sydney on my stopover in Kuala Lumpur. She seemed happy enough to hear from me. And burst out laughing when I said where I was phoning from. 'You're where?' she asked. I said Kula Lumpur and as most of you will know it is pronounced 'Kala Lumper'. 'You mean 'Kooala Lumpuuur,' she purred.

I said, 'I think not! Ask any Brit'.

She said, 'Ask any Canadian'.

Which was just the start of many varied pronunciations of things in our household.

And that was it. The start of a most wonderful relationship, no matter the age difference, no matter how she pronounces things. We laugh, even through the very tough times, we always find a way to laugh.

We started a long distance relationship, which had Niki setting up courses in Toronto where she was the Wellness Coordinator for Nokia Canada, every month or so. I went over the first time in late 2000 and we had a great time and I was hooked. Herself on the other hand, was a bit more wary.

I was home a week from my first visit to Toronto and Niki called me.

'Neil, this is great, but before this goes any further, you've got to sort your situation out. I'll be here if you can do that.' That honesty, and her trust in me to get myself sorted was the start of something amazing. The cloud was lifting, even if ever so slightly.

As I say, it's everything I ever wanted in a relationship,

with Niki. We have two beautiful girls together, Brooke and Taylor, and everything works well with Ashley. In fact, Alison met her perfect fella around the same time I met Niki. I'm delighted to say Ashley gets on really well with Lloyd, Alison's husband and Niki. He's such a good son. He could have made it a real nightmare for both his mum and I with our respective new partners, but he didn't and I love him dearly for that.

Within a dysfunctional marriage you don't see your damage, and you don't understand the challenges waiting for you. I was very lucky in that I was able to face those with Niki. Because believe me, when I did get my situation sorted and we got together… well! Things sped up. Within 6 months Niki said 'My contract ends in May. I don't own a house or have kids of my own. But you have a job to finish with Ashley. I'll move to the UK.'

I had moved out the house by then and I was on my own. Niki came to live with me in May 2001 and we were the start of an awesome team.

There were still difficulties though. Any change is going to make some ripples. When Niki first came over, we were actually living in my bedsit for a bit. The arrangement that had been made between Alison and me, was that Alison wanted to have the house for Ashley's sake, to maintain familiarity in an already difficult time, and we would have the club. I wish I had looked more into it and thought about the long term implications of giving up the house, as the club finances and everything that was tied to it, were worse than I knew. That rashness really put Niki and I behind the eight ball as it were, as we had no money and only the club, which was not only in debt, but needed a massive makeover. Finances just weren't what I did at the club, it wasn't on my radar, and I wanted it all done and dusted. I just wanted to get on with things and on with my life.

However, I should have made it a point to know. It would have made our start, Niki and I, so much easier. However, Ashley was going to be comfortable, so that was the main thing, and Niki and I had a plan based on her Corporate Wellness work in Canada, so, optimistically, we thought we could turn it all around. We had the club and we took it over as a business however dying it was.

The fact of the matter was now we didn't have a house and were really struggling as our income was based on the club. We took on a business partner and that input helped for a while, to the degree we thought we could start looking for our first house together. We found a lovely cottage in Brinklow, not far from Rugby and not far from Coventry where I promised to stay close enough to help with Ashley.

After our bid on that house fell through, (we call it gazumping here in the UK, where you put in an offer and it's accepted, until another, better offer comes in last second) we found ourselves homeless as we had given in our letting notice on the bedsit.

Our only option was the office in the club. We rolled out a foam mattress in the office after lock up every night and rolled it back up every morning ready to open for business. It was a difficult start but it pushed us to wrap our head around what we were going to do and to redirect again. Talk about trial by fire! Again, it was that bounce back situation. We weren't going to be put down and we were going to work our way back. That old saying I've mentioned before about how the secret of Judo success is if you are thrown seven times you get up eight? We were getting back up. Again. Only this time we were doing it together.

So, for the first time in a long time I had a rock solid emotional foundation. I knew I did when Niki first told me we were expecting. Funny thing was that it was one of the very first questions she asked me in Sydney, once I had told her about my home life. She asked if I wanted to have more children and up until that point, I hadn't given it much thought. Alison and I had talked about it of course, years before, when Ashley was young but there again, the subject got shuffled to the back and not really pursued. I think subconsciously, we both knew it wasn't on the cards and that the situation wasn't meant to be.

I told Niki, that yes, I could see being a father again as I love being one so much and had a fleeting twinge of sadness for what hadn't been. I don't know if it was that sentiment that made me say yes, or the thought that it was a make or break question, if you know what I mean, but it did get me thinking.

The summer that Niki had moved to the UK, she became very ill. She would double over with abdominal pains, get sweats and get dizzy. We were at her parents in Selkirk, Canada at the time and everyone was giving each other the knowing looks but at the same time concerned for her well-being.

As soon as we got home to Coventry, she went in to see the doctor. Now you're asking why didn't we get a pregnancy test and just get it sorted then and there. I know. But she was insistent that she wasn't pregnant and that the change in her birth control pill was to blame. As we drove to the doctors, though, her expression started to change from concern to a bit of whimsical, 'So what if I am pregnant, Neil?' she blurted out.

Then she shook her head dismissing the idea, 'No, it's the worst timing ever! We live in our office, for Christ sakes!'

And with that her face changed back to resolute, with a touch of concern, if not a wisp of whimsy.

She asked if I was coming in to the doctor's as we parked in the surgery car park.

'No, I'll wait here for you.'

I don't know why I didn't go in. I think I was scared to be honest. I just sat there with my thumbs tapping on the steering wheel to a non-existent beat. Then the passenger's door opened and in popped Niki. With a big outward breath, she told me we weren't expecting. We both just sat there for quite a while, both looking out the front windscreen, letting the news sink in.

'I mean that's good right?' she asked finally turning to me. 'Yes, it's not the right time' nodding my head, '… is it?'

We moped around the club for 2 weeks, not sure of what was wrong with us, Niki had received a new prescription for a new type of pill and ironically the doctor said handing it to her, 'try this one. That is, if that's what you really want?'

She hadn't fulfilled the prescription and it got to the point that she had to or the decision was going to be taken out of our hands completely. She asked me why I had been so down these last couple of weeks and I turned it on her: why had she?

She took a big breath in and told me that she was sad about the test, that she wasn't expecting to be, she wanted to be thankful we had 'dodged that bullet' as it were, but found that she wasn't. She was pretty sad.

The whole time she was talking she didn't look at me, I guess because she was nervous of my reaction to her revelation. She did finally turn to look at me. I could feel myself smile for the first time in 2 weeks. Niki then started to smile which then turned into a big grin.
'Well I guess that's decided then.'

To think back on it, it was amazing. It still is. Niki has brought things out of me and has helped me to develop things I was good at but took for granted or just assumed that everyone knew it too.

I have an incredible brain in some ways; I will forget my dental appointment but I can remember things and dissect things from years ago. It's an analytical mind-set that's helped me a lot with Judo. It's also means I dwell, sometimes, and for too long, on things I shouldn't. Niki is so good at getting things out of me, redirecting that analytical mind-set into building new things, not dwelling and obsessing over why old ones fell over. Learn, then move on, she says.

Saying that, with new management comes new ideas , however, the business was too far gone and we were running at a loss. The Academy was finished and we were concentrating on the health club side of things. Front of House management became a real problem as loyalties to Alison made line managing a real task, to the point of having to let some personnel go. It was made clear to the staff that these were the changes necessary to bring the standards up again, and if they could not see themselves as being a part of that team, then maybe it was best for everyone that they find somewhere more appropriate.

Ok, maybe it wasn't quite said like that, but that was the meaning behind it. I'm sure as the new manager came head to head with Alison's manageress, this was what he had in mind at the time.

Needless to say, the manageress left in a state and only came back to serve us with tribunal papers. Her words of, 'it's nothing personal' still makes me shake my head, if not grimace a little at the thought of the perspective of some people. Alison and I helped her a lot while she worked at the club, while she was a single parent, but this didn't seem to make any difference to her.

When the dust settled on that wave of disappointment to the tune of a few thousand pounds, we started to really look closely at the membership numbers, which on paper looked like close to 400. So why wasn't the club sustaining? On closer inspection, we were shocked to discover that only 80 standing order members were being paid at the time. Again, the lack of business managing skills and experience did us in, and should have been brought up during the tribunal. However, I know my weaknesses and that was the financial and administrative side of things. It's the reason I agreed to a business partnership, to look after and make stronger those skills that I'm not personally an expert in.

It was because of this revelation on the accounts that it

was decided that a dedicated person be put in charge of the management of the accounts, the banking and the general financial running of the club. An Office Manager was needed. The successful candidate was likable, amiable, laid back, and in contrast to the last employee, now ex employee, a fresh breeze of reasonableness. What we didn't realise at the time was that what laid beneath this particular easy-going, smiley person was a thick layer of deception and calculation of how to really use my club for her own personal gain.

The embezzlement only came to light because of a charity called Baby Lifeline, who inadvertently threw us a lifeline as well. Our business partner, Tony, called us all in for a meeting stating he had some dire news. He had recently been contacted by Baby Lifeline asking if we had any recommendations for an Office Manager. As ours was only part time and we couldn't afford to give her any more hours, Tony suggested that she work for them part time. After a few months, the chairperson again contacted Tony, however, now to recommend to him that we check our accounts very carefully.

Contrary to Baby Lifeline's successful charitable intake, our intake was quite small and we easily overlooked that small amounts had been filtered into her own account. This, at a time Niki and I didn't have enough for groceries, as well as her being pregnant with Brooke. When we did find out that money was going out of the account, and we traced it to her, I remember saying to Niki that I had to find out why.

Why would she embezzle money from us, when she knew how difficult things were and still steal from us? When I phoned her mobile, I didn't for one second think she would pick up. However, after the courteous 3 rings, a very cold, calm voice said, 'Hello Neil.'

'Why?' I said, 'Why me? Why take from me? You know how hard it is for us right now.'

She said to me in a matter of fact way, 'Don't take it personally, Neil. I just need the money to pay for my house and my car. I want a big house, and I want a big car. You need money for that.'

I could do nothing but put the phone down and blink at Niki who was stood there with me. I think it was the cold heartedness that surprised me most.

This was just another thing to add to the long list of experiences that would help us grow a thicker skin for the future. However, with the arrival of Brooke and our need for a bigger home to house both the baby and Ashley when he visited, we needed to start thinking of other pathways. We were living in Kenilworth now and loved it immensely, however, had no way of making the jump to the next level of house that we would need. We would need to look outside Kenilworth, and for that matter, outside Warwickshire. To do this, we needed out of the club as well.

Top: Furze Bans - Wooden house sign
Bottom: Rugby

12. Rugby & Wales – A Whole Different Ball Game

The challenge then became building a professional career instead of the club. We both realised that the coaching side of our work needed something definite, a direction of its own.

After the 1996 Olympic Games in Atlanta and the disaster that everybody experienced at those Olympics I suspected that the BJA would be reviewing my position. In the past, the British Judo Association have never been good at looking after their former fighters and staff and this was no exception. Of course questions needed to be asked as to why we had such a disastrous Olympic Games but just sacking the team manager without anything else in place is not the answer.

What they did was to move me sidewards to a position called Technical Advisor, which, I knew and everybody knew, basically meant they were preparing me for the sack. It was a normal occurrence for British Judo, to sack the Team Manager on return from the Olympic Games. They had done it many times before even after medals have been won. I guess I should have considered myself lucky that, in my case, it wasn't straight away.

The Technical Advisor's position meant regular trips around the country to different clubs and then ended at Bisham Abbey in 2003/4 where they set up a full time educational program for developing Judoka. This position went on for longer than I thought it would. I really think the BJA just didn't know what to do with me, but didn't want to let me go either, with the very real possibility of me going rogue.

It was very hard on Niki with our new daughter, Brooke, and not only with all the travelling, but always with the cloud over our heads of the possibility of losing my job.

The club was no longer making any money at all and we were in a position that I needed to release my time, which was often 12 hours a day at the club and making no money at the end of it. The club and the full-time program had run its course with many of the full timers changing direction with their careers and the health club side of the business having no chance of survival with so much opposition from the surrounding clubs.

We had to decide how best to utilise my time and make money at the same time. We were making no money at the club at all and so we decided that the best thing to do was to sell the club.

This was a really difficult decision as we had many friends and colleagues who relied on the club for different reasons but in the end we had to think about ourselves, and our family. Tony Weaver, who had been helping us with a vested interest for a while now offered to buy the club from us.

It was at this time that we found the beautiful house where we are living today near Rugby and decided to sell our house in Kenilworth. Niki loved the house in Kenilworth, which was a small terraced house. It had beautiful décor and a character that we will never forget. It was our first house together and we had many happy times there, but we needed something bigger. Our family was getting bigger and we wanted a garden for Brooke.

It's in our nature to take chances, so it was no surprise that Furze Barns caught our eye. Committing to the house in Rugby, which really is an on-going project of renovation, in order to take our housing situation to the next level, seemed normal. I had done it before, I could do it again. And it was ironic that I found myself back at my birthplace and that of my father's.

We bought two plots on an old farm, which were really part of a group of barns, and were perfect for our needs. We bought one barn for the business side, housing our gym and office, and the main building, which includes the 400 year old cottage for our living quarters. There are two buildings that we still have to renovate but I did say it was an on-going project.

Everything seemed nicely set. As always, Niki and I were pushing forwards and trying to make things better and carve a nice little livelihood and home in the Northamptonshire countryside, when we got hit with the bombshell we somehow always knew was threatening.

The BJA contacted me in November to tell me that I've been sacked. Ok they'll say 'made redundant'. The stigma behind being sacked is one thing but being canned for no good reason was what rankled most. Yet again I was going to have to dig in in order to survive. That old saying again: if you fall down seven times you get up eight. I think it's a Chinese proverb, and for Niki and I there is never a truer saying.

I can remember the call. I was bathing Brooke, while Niki was fixing dinner. Niki came in with the phone saying it was the BJA.
'Hey! You alright?' I said to the familiar voice on the phone.

That was the last thing I said for a good 5 minutes while the familiar voice explained to me what was about to happen.

I broke my silence, 'What am I supposed to do? I've just bought a house, we've got Brooke now!'

'I'm sorry, Neil but you'll be fine. You always land on your feet.' Came the answer through the phone.

'I have no other income, now. You! You, my friend, have

just lost me my house!'

I put the phone down on another apology whispered down the line, and looked up at Niki who was standing in the doorway.

'Well, we knew that was coming, didn't we?' I said.

'It's not fair, Neil. We've been asking for months what was happening. If we should be looking for something else, for just a head's up on things to get ourselves sorted. We should've have known when we couldn't get a straight answer.'

I knew my line manager knew something was changing. I could smell it. I could feel it. Something just wasn't quite right. All my questions, veiled and straight out were being ignored and waved aside. Well, now I knew why.

Yet again we were going to have to reassess our lives and I was going to have to look for work. I had always had a steady stream of courses at clubs but we needed something on a more regular basis giving us a financial foundation. Niki was pregnant again with our second daughter, Taylor and was due in September.

When I think about how I felt when I was given a £5000 send off from the BJA, looking back I wish that I had pushed for more. Surely I was worth more than that after everything that I had done for British Judo? I have always supported British Judo, promoted British Judo, and still promote not only British Judo, but Judo all over the world.

Niki and I started to look for other positions within the UK. A position ironically with the BJA did come up, soon after, and I was asked by them to apply for the job. I still was smarting from the last knife in the back, but what could I do? I needed to gain a regular income. I applied, made the shortlist and was asked to come in for an interview.

I think I surprised the panel with my presentation as they kept stating afterwards that it was more than they thought I had to offer.

Someone mumbled that 'this was going to be harder then we thought.' Which I thought was a strange thing to say at the time, but I took it as a compliment and a sign that I was in with a good chance.

I wasn't offered the job of Coach Education Director for the British Judo Association. In fact, I found I was only one of 2 candidates on the 'shortlist'. I wouldn't be surprised if there had been only the 2 applicants. I was just asked to make the process look more credible.

The call I received from the BJA to tell me I was unsuccessful for the Coach Educator's position was literally a double edged sword. No, I was not successful on this occasion, however, they would really like me to consider applying for the Head Coach position at the Scottish Institute of Sport in Stirling.

I said I would consider it, however, wanted assurance that this was not just another decorated shortlist; that I had a bona fide shot at the position. I didn't want to waste my time if they had somebody already in mind.

When I applied for the Scottish position of Head Coach, I was assured that it was indeed somewhere where they, the BJA, wanted me to be, to be a part of the overall performance structure, where my technical expertise could be put to good use.

When I interviewed for the position, and I walked away from the interview, I had the feeling that this was not the case. We had to submit a remuneration, how much we wanted for the position. Niki had done the maths and sent me on my way North stating, 'don't take anything less than £50k'.

I put in £40k thinking this would help my situation. It didn't. I received the call while working out my leave at Bisham Abbey a week later. They were sorry. I made an excellent candidate, however, it made more financial sense to them to offer the position to the other 2 candidates, one of which they could laterally transfer from another position, and hire the other at half the remuneration I had presented. I had been beaten not only by one candidate but by both candidates. Not a great ego boost to say the least. How did that relationship of two leaders turn out? Well let's just say you can't have 2 leaders as I found out in my coaching partnership in 1996. But that's their own books to write, and from what I have heard, I dare say they would make interesting reading.

I was now beside myself and I didn't know what to do in order to make money for my family. It got to the stage where I decided to sign on for government benefits so that we could get some financial help. I found that this was one of the most difficult things that I had ever had to do. Of course, people who find themselves at the Job Centre are a mix of those desperately wanting to work and would do anything to do so, and others that were clearly sponging off the system.

What really did it for Niki, and myself was this one time when she decided to come with me to the Job Centre as we had to pick up groceries and baby stuff. Seated beside Niki and Brooke on the waiting bench was one woman surrounded by her many children.

She was being badgered for money for ice creams and sweets. She fished in her pocket and took out a wad of notes, peeled three off to give to her kids, asking them to get her some cigarettes at the same time. Niki just stared at her and then looked around to me. She got up, walked out the door and I could see her head in hands, standing outside on the pavement, sobbing.

I think this just made us more determined to do it ourselves and I vowed never to step foot in that place again. Not because it was the Job Centre but because yet again we felt that the system was letting us down. I think in life each person has to accept the cards that are dealt to them, but once they're in hand, we have to decide how to play those cards in order to win the game.

This is, of course, easier if your hand has all the necessary information. It was difficult not to think that there was a conspiracy afoot in order to stop me working in the UK and that some people would've been glad to see the back of me. It was at this time that the Welsh Judo Association invited me to Cardiff to run a seminar for them. Little did I know that it was really an interview for the Head Coach position.

Ironically, Niki had seen the advert a couple of weeks before and jokingly had said, 'Well there's still Wales!'

And we did consider it for a time, but it was only offering £30K, which didn't make it very attractive when we had to consider the amount of hours and the fact we would have sell the house and move down to Wales.

After finishing the seminar in Cardiff, I was approached by some of the Welsh executive and asked if I would be interested in the National Coach's position. I remember coming home in the car and phoning Niki, as I always did coming home from a course, and telling her that I had a job, if I wanted it.

I was later to learn that the conspiracy continued to Wales as a call was made to the Welsh Chairman at the time, telling him 'that it wasn't in their best interest to employ me.' Luckily, the Welsh Executive decided against the implied threat and took me on and I owe them a lot for that.

It was a great opportunity and with a great bunch of people and athletes. It was a great platform to show that I really did know what I was talking about and those who wanted to work and work hard demonstrated the immediate progression that could be made with technical work and strategies. We started to really make a mark on the British

Judo scene.

The position in Wales was a great job for me as it enabled me to instruct to the grassroots, as well as with the Welsh National Team, and gave me the opportunity to develop another group of youngsters with a system within a national structure. I had so much support in Wales and worked very closely with Keven Williams who has become one of my closest friends. He supported many of my decisions and was there to help and support me when I needed it. I will never forget him being there for Niki and I, always there with advice and support.

The only problem with it, of course, was that for the next year I commuted from the farmhouse in Rugby to Cardiff every week and spent much of my time away from my family. Our family life is very special to us and in the end Niki said that she hadn't signed up for this: looking after 2 small children on her own, and we needed to think about moving to Cardiff.

And that's just what we did, that November of 2006, we moved to a house on an estate in Brackla, outside of Bridgend. It was in between the WIS at Cardiff and another centre we started in Swansea at Alan Petherbridge's club. We chose there due to his pedigree and the respect that all Welsh Judoka have for Alan. We wanted it to be part of his legacy.

Brooke had already started school at the local village school in Yelvertoft, Northamptonshire, and only after 6 weeks there, she was placed at Brackla Infants School, which was a really great school, as well as Yelvertoft had been. So we were very lucky on that front. Taylor was 2 years old and was a firm favourite with the younger team members who I think saw her as a type of mascot!

We once again were taking massive steps forwards as part of our survival and my partner was, as always, gave me 360 support. The decision we had to make was what to do with the house in Rugby as it was unfinished, unconverted, and we had a massive mortgage. The obvious thing would be to rent the house out and cover the mortgage. Either that or sell the house. The problem was it was unfit to rent out but was a great time to sell the house. We would have to renovate it whether we were to rent it or sell it.

We did have a buyer, straight away, luckily. A young couple with the same vision we had had when we bought it. It all looked great and much needed, as paying both a mortgage in Rugby and rent in Brackla was starting to take its toll severely. We made a deal with the buyers who had yet to sell their property, that instead of a deposit, to take the property off the market, they would pay our mortgage until they sold their house. Such was the price we were going to get for it! Luck was shining down on us finally!

Spring turned to summer and summer turned to autumn and still no sale on the buyer's property. Everyone was getting a bit anxious.

One early afternoon in November, coming home from training at the WIS, I walked in the front door to see Niki sitting on the stairs.

'What's wrong, Babe?' She had been crying, I could tell.

'They've pulled out. They can't afford the house anymore. The estate agent just called.'

So normally, the house just goes back up on the market and you start again. That works fine when it's not 4 weeks before Christmas and on the brink of another house market crash, one that the UK hasn't seen since 1990.

2007 saw the housing market reach an all time low and houses were going up for sale everywhere as people were trying not to go bankrupt. The banks had even reached their limit of re-possessions and were selling houses as soon as they repossessed them, at a loss, leaving people with massive loans to repay. We tried for a while. We really stretched ourselves to maintain both properties. We realised that people were not taking on 'projects', so we started to renovate just enough to make it look attractive for the selling market.

Niki started commuting back and forth for days at a time to do the renovations while I did the trainings and looked after the girls. By April, it was ready for market and there it sat. It sat on the market for over a year, having loads of viewings but still too much of a project for most people. Those who did want a project were asking ridiculously low prices and wouldn't cover what we owed. We couldn't keep going like this. We had to cut it loose. What I had said to the BJA on that call a year ago was now coming true. I was going to lose my house. The only asset, really that we had.

***

As far as the job in Wales was concerned I learnt a great deal on how to structure programs, develop teams and work with governing bodies that supported me. It was refreshing and gave me renewed faith in systems. The icing on the cake during our stay in Wales was that Niki was offered a position as General Manager for Welsh Judo and things were really starting to look up. The only problem was of course that we were both working all hours and were not spending enough time together. It was keenly felt because we have such a close marriage and incredible family.

One way we combatted this was we started taking Friday afternoons for ourselves, once Taylor started at the Infant school. We would take advantage of the time to explore the area such as Ogmore Beach and Castle, the city of Cardiff and its castle, Magram Park, to Porthcawl renting kayaks for the afternoon, and out west and up into the valleys for some sensational walks. We really did enjoy our time there.

Some of our best Easter holidays were in Wales. Everyone scooted off to Spain or Portugal, but as finances dictated, we elected to stay in Wales and explore. One Easter we went west to St David's and Pembrokeshire, ending up on Tenby Beach where we got sunburned! Turned out it was raining in Spain, (mainly on the plain, so I hear!) Another time, we weaved up to North Wales and found Bala Lake where Ashley joined us for a few days, taking in the steam trains, kayaking and hill walks.

I had my 50th Birthday in Wales in the September and it is one I will always remember as I was surrounded by my friends from near and far, Judo and non Judo, doing the things I love to do. Niki arranged a house up in Bala, as we had liked it so much there, to rent for the weekend and jammed the whole weekend full of outdoor activities that people could come and join in as they pleased.

We went white water rafting, to walking the back hills, with a party at the local pub. Stan, the Man, Cantrill was our DJ and Niki with her good friend Jenny Crawford baked a caked that must have been 2 feet tall. How they got it to the pub I'll never know. Friends from Scotland, Wales, England & Canada were there to help me celebrate, but my first thing was to soak it all up. I had been travelling so much at that point with the team, and I was pretty tired. I remember Niki showing me which bedroom was ours, and I thought I would just lie down, listen to the stream pass underneath the window. That was the last thing I remember until Niki called up saying people were arriving. I have to say it was one time I can remember feeling totally and completely relaxed and calm. A great way to start my 5th decade.

When we returned from our festivities up North, Niki asked me, 'Ok, you're 50 now. What is it you want to do in the next 5 years? What unfinished business do you have that we should strive for in these next few years?'

I had to sit there and ponder this a bit. Let's face it, the last time I did this, it was a huge turning point. What I said to Niki was that I would like to have another crack at producing an Olympic champion. Even though I had contributed to many Olympic medallists throughout the years it would still have been nice to have taken somebody all the way there.

This was when the chance in Belgium came about.

Actually, I was in Belgium for a Judo competition and was approached in a similar fashion as the way I was approached in Wales. The Belgians approached me asking if I knew of anybody that would be interested in the Belgian Team Manager's position. What they were really asking was if I might be available for the position. And I guess I was, technically speaking, as my contract with Welsh Judo was coming to an end in March. Up until then I had assumed that it would just roll over into another 4 year contract.

But then it hit me.

The realisation that I hadn't yet been approached to renew my contract with Welsh Judo, suddenly hit me between the eyes. You would think I would learn after all this time not to assume, but here I was again. I had to make a decision before it was made for me... again.

It came down to money, really, which I guess in most cases it does. I didn't really want to leave what I had started in Wales, as I thought it was going rather well and here was somewhere I could really make my mark. I had to look at Niki though as well. She was drowning in her position as General Manager. Her mum, Pam, took me aside one visit and likened it to watching a train crash. She was concerned, as was I. Niki is a very capable woman and you do assume that she has it all together as she does get things done. But I did have to ask myself, if this really was the case. She was promoted swiftly from Office Manager to General Manager when the previous husband and wife team left, leaving her with both positions of Office & General Manager to deal with. We had to put the NAEF Coach Education business on hold as we just didn't have the time. The amount of work of the two positions, two young daughters and essentially looking after me and my fragile state, (as I hadn't employed any coping strategies other than drink, at this point) soon led to too much for her to handle.

Her health was floundering and her normally smiling face was now a rarity. Her mum was right. She was a train wreck ready to happen. And it did. She went to the doctors where she broke down and was immediately signed off on stress leave.

In fact, this is how I was dragged in from the dark ages into the computer age. Until then, I had just written everything with pen and paper and had someone else type it up. Hey! I know how to work to my strengths!

Niki was having none of it. She sat me down in front of a laptop and stated from 'now on' I would have to type up my own reports. It must have been purgatory for her, in fact I know it was. The first day of my (tap)… (search, ah yes there it is)… (tap)… (search)… (tap) keyboarding skills, she looked up from her work, gave a strangled cry, grabbed her work and fled the room. But I learned quite quickly, especially how to save my work.

My first report took me all day, I mean hours. It was 2 pages long and I could tell Niki was screaming inside, putting up with all my swearing and out loud, heavy sighing directed at the screen, but knowing not to interfere if I was to learn how to do this. Then it happened. Poof! A blank screen. My hands flew into my hair, 'What's that?! What just happened?!'

Niki heaved a controlled sigh, 'Now what?'

'It's gone. It's vanished. Where would it go? Just help me find it! Please!'

'Ok, hold on. Don't panic. It's Windows so each screen is like a window, Neil. You've probably clicked on the screen and covered it up with another. Let's have a look. Is this it?'

'No.'

'This it?'

'No.'

'What about this one?'

'No.'

'Hmmm, ok.' I could tell she was starting to worry a little, 'Where did you save it to?'

'Save it? What do you mean save it?'

'Neil, you saved the document to the disk drive, right?'

'Nik, what does that mean? I have no idea what you just

said? You have to save? What? Like in a safe?'

'Oh dear God,' she moaned.

Niki then went on to not only tell me, but show me what saving a document is all about. I had just spent 4 hours on this with nothing to show for it. I slammed my way out of the house, swearing the place down. Needless to say, I did return some time later to re-write my report. Me and the *Save* icon are the best of buddies now.

Amelie Rosseneu and Neil at the Under 23 European final

13. Belgium –The Best Beer I Never Tasted

Niki's stress leave gave her the breather she needed to work through things and decide on what she wanted to do next. The Belgium thing was on the table, however Niki had lived for some time in The Netherlands in 1992, not far from where we would be stationed, and did not have fond memories of the area. However, she did say that her Judo club and coach were the saving graces.

Being the very practical woman that she is, she worked it out and found that the new position in Belgium would be a considerable amount more than our combined salaries, there, in Wales. It would mean that it would free her time to work on our NAEF business, building up the name and creating a brand and in essence re-launching the name: Neil Adams. It would also be a good chance to re build our financial state. She liked the idea of the girls and possibly herself learning a new language and it all seemed to point to the next logistical step.

At the beginning of the negotiations, the new Performance Director of the VJF (Vlaamse Judo Federatie) came over to London to talk me into taking the job. Of course, it would mean moving to Belgium, renting accommodation and relocating the girls into Belgian schools. It was a big decision for Niki and I, to decide whether to find an International school in Belgium or throw them in the deep end so that they could learn another language and a new culture. It was Niki really who convinced me that total immersion into the language was the only way to go from her experience living in Montreal.

We decided to go for it. This meant leaving a successful system I helped to create in Wales. This helped them get a brand new dojo, which we were instrumental in designing with Keven Williams and the management at the WIS. Typical! A brand new dojo on the way, and just how I would like a dojo, and I decide to move. It's like finally renovating a house, not for you, but to sell to someone else, for someone else's use and enjoyment. You get it just the way you want it, and then you leave. Worse yet, not getting an invite to the 'house warming' was a bit of sore point as well. But hey, like I said before, with new management, comes new ideas.

It wasn't an easy decision, family-wise either. Leaving Ashley, who was now finished university looking towards his adult future, and my mum and dad in Devon made it a really difficult decision, especially at their stage in life. We were going to be away for 3 ½ years but it would give us a chance to improve our financial position, really sink our teeth into NAEF, the coach education business we had put on hold, and to possibly rescue our house in England. I started the position in April and commuted between the UK and Belgium until Niki and the girls joined me in July. We found a lovely modern house in Sint Job in 't Goor, near Antwerp, which was close to the training centre and had a big garden with a pool, so the girls were sold.

One of the obstacles, other than the heated politics of Vlaamse v Wallonie, and personal coaches, was that I had a good situation with the International Judo Federation (IJF) commentating at their Grand Prix and Grand Slam tournaments that were Olympic qualification events. The world tour was in its infancy and I, fortunately was there at the beginning. It was a great opportunity for me as a commentator. After meetings with the IJF, the VJF agreed to let me do both jobs when I was away so I was both team trainer for part of the competition and, commentator for the other part. If one of the fighters got through to the final stages then I was allowed by the IJF to coach my fighter and then run directly to the commentary position. When I look back now it was a tall order but it seemed to work really well.

The girls went into the Belgian school system and immediately had to start learning Flemish, a dialect of Dutch. In fact, all their lessons were in Flemish and their friends didn't speak a word of English. It was so difficult for them for the first six months, however, after that something changed. They not only started to speak the language, but they also adapted to the culture and they started to make lots of friends. Brooke and Taylor became fluent in Flemish and in fact, Taylor, although she could speak English, could only read and write in Flemish.

Looking back it was a difficult decision to make, but it gave them a second language and for that we're grateful. Even though we were starting to settle in Belgium, the hours that I had to work were far more then we bargained for. I was away every weekend at either a World Cup, European Cup, a Grand Prix or Grand Slam tournament as well as World Championships. And then there were the week-long training camps on top of that. I was tired all the time. I would return from an event on the Monday night and have to be on the mat at the school on the Tuesday morning at 8am. I'd teach that week until I left with the team that Friday for another event. It really is a young man's game, and yes, I have a hard time saying that, but it's true.

It's a bit of an oxymoron, really. To have success, you need experience. With age, comes experience, but so does life with family commitments. The job calls for a lot of travel, which if you're young, and you don't have the family commitments, this suits the schedule, but you don't have the necessary experience. I've seen many, many marriages and relationships of friends and colleagues go down the tubes because of this job, and most likely my first one included.

If I could go back and renegotiate, it would have been for the position of Technical Director or something of that nature. It is where my strengths are. My mandate would be to increase the technical skills of athletes and the coaches. I think that is where Federations will have to go in the future anyway in order to save the sport.

I'm not saying my mat-side skills are non-existent. I have been known to turn a few important matches around, creating championship titles. However, at this time in my life, and with a young family again, I don't want to travel so much. Maybe, as the girls are coming to an interesting age of teenage-hood, they will be more interested in travelling with me. I really hope I can make that happen. Nothing would please me more.

The house situation in England never went away. We were half hoping that it would sort itself out and that maybe the bank would solve our problems for us. The mortgage was accumulating and we were getting further and further into debt.

We still had the fight with the bank regarding the house. We had no idea what to do with it and called the bank to make a deal. They refused it. They didn't want the house as they already had too many on their books!

Great!!

Just great!!

Can't even *give* the house away. What a position to be in. We kept doing this dance for a few months until the bank did decide to repossess the house. It was a nerve-wracking day. Knowing at 10am that the bailiffs were going to be at the door of the house changing locks. We were pacing the floor with 30 minutes to go and suddenly Niki stood dead still and said, 'I can't do it!' and she picked up her phone.

Within 5 minutes she had made a deal with the banks, paid some money towards the house, and the bailiffs were called off. What possessed her to do it? I don't think either one of us will ever know. It was just instinct.

It was at this stage that we had to decide what to do. We

owed money everywhere due to the mortgage, renting in Wales, renting in Belgium, renovations in Rugby, you name it. We had completely dug ourselves a hole, ironically trying to keep our heads above water. Unfortunately, the only real option was bankruptcy. It was time to draw a line.

Most things owing, we found, were in my name, so it was me that had to take the hit. Niki could then continue to trade and work the business, continuing on with our goal. Of course it made sense on paper. That didn't mean my heart and ego didn't take a right good beating. In fact, it was one of the saddest times of my life. I remember the judge looking down from his high seat and saying to me, 'Do you understand exactly what this entails?'

'Yes, sir.'

But I didn't. Not really.

The stigma that comes with going bankrupt is as black as the hole you have found yourself in. Especially for someone who is used to winning, this was a no-win situation and hard to see how it was the best thing to do at the time. The ramifications of having your credit rating hit, for someone who is not a big business man, is dire. You can't get a credit card, your bank accounts are all set back to the simplest form, like a teenager's, so purchasing anything online is very difficult. My name was no longer on the house and I couldn't finance a car. In fact, there were very few things I could do. These restrictions have stayed with me for 7 years, however, it has hemmed in our financial plans and we have learned a great lesson from it all. We have built up the business without loans or overdrafts and have had to think things through very carefully and maybe not as impulsively as before.

So with that stewing in the background and keeping Niki busy with building the coach education business, I turned my energies to the men and woman of the VJF Judo team. We had the Olympics qualifications to prepare for. And a lot of preparation was needed, as these athletes were young. Many had just finished their Junior careers and were now stepping into the Senior ranks.

For the most part, the personal coaches were very helpful and accommodating. They trusted my methods and my programming. That is except two. These two coaches were against me from the beginning and I was warned they would be. It was suspected they wanted, if not the job itself, the money that funded the position.

A foreigner in Belgium was almost unheard of so they were on a mission to get me out from the very beginning.

That December I played into their hands perfectly and gave them the needed ammunition. One of coaches at the school and myself brought a team to England in two minibuses for a Christmas training camp. In between trainings, the coach and I went out for a Christmas drink and had too much. We definitely crossed the line. We couldn't remember where our accommodation was and had to call one of the fighters for directions. It immediately got back to VJF Head Office that we had been drinking and we were brought in front of the Executive Committee on our return from England.

The two personal coaches were right on it, pushing for our resignation. The other coach was sacked and I remember looking at the faces interrogating me. I studied those faces looking at me. The disappointment on their faces went straight to my bone marrow, and I realised right then how so disappointed I was in myself.

I told myself that this would never happen again and said as much to the Committee and that I would apologise personally to the team. On the way back from Zele to home I phoned Niki and I explained what had happened. I promised her that I was going to stop drinking and that it would never happen again.

Niki was, at first, dubious as she had heard it before, but asked if I wanted any professional help. I said, 'No, I can do this alone.'

And I did.

From that second on, the second when I decided to stop, my life changed and I saw things in a different light. It was no longer fuzzy. Everything is clearer and I'm able to focus much better. I am a much better husband, father and, I dare say, man.

And with most things, it takes an event to trigger things, to trigger change. People can stand in front of you, physically shake you and it won't change how you feel or act. In fact, in my case, when people say 'Go left', I'll purposely go right.

I've always been that.

You may say that reverse psychology would be the key, but I've always had my own mind and will do what I want to do, regardless, and sometimes cutting off my nose to spite my face, as the saying goes, just for the pure principle and the permission to say, I did it my way.

Most times, if not all, there needs to be a reason to change and that, more often than not, comes in the form of an event.

Whether you want to change the way you look, either by losing weight or gaining weight, or want to be healthier or fitter, stop the stress in your job, so are looking to change career paths; to stop smoking, drugs, eating indulgence, or as in my case, drinking. Unfortunately, we seem to need something catastrophic to snap us out of it, and then into it: into change. Thankfully, mine wasn't a heart attack, or my second marriage going down the tubes, or someone being injured, or worse. In the grand scheme of things, it really was just a 'polite' reminder of what I had, what I had achieved and what I had yet to give. I had to change things to save these things precious to me: love of my family, my hard-earned reputation, and my legacy: how I want to be remembered.

The changes started when I called all the athletes together for a meeting and delivered the sincerest apology I could muster. I wanted them to know they could trust me. I wanted them to know that I was truly sorry for putting my ghosts before their well being. They needed to know that I was on their side and that I wanted their success just as much as they did.

They were great. If anything it cemented the group. Some tears were shed, mostly out of relief I suspect and now I was totally focused on the job at hand. And that was getting them ready for international competition and to make a mark on international Judo.

So, I had work to do. I needed to find out exactly what I was working with here in Belgium, not just float through training. I needed to know what level they were working at when they weren't with me, and I needed to know what their commitment to the programme was. I interviewed each team member individually to find out what training they were doing, how many times a week they were training, what skills training they were doing, and how many randoris per week they did.

What was interesting was that when you took away the normal club practice against normal club people from the amount of quality randoris that they did, it was fewer than 20 per week. I pointed out that when training for the Olympic Games or World Championships, large periods of my training included 70 quality randoris each week. These were in Japan or training camps. This was a minimum. For them to progress they would have to increase their practice time, the *quality* of their training and show me that they were going to give it 100% commitment.

To my delight I had a select group that did just that and soon started to shine through. Every morning I was teaching at Kattenbrooke, the training school on the outskirts of Antwerp, which included their education with Judo training. The school was excellent and started a lot of cadets and juniors on their way giving them a good skills base for the future.

What I noticed immediately, however, was that this school only catered for four years preparation and then left each student to their own devices after the four years. What I wanted was the second four years. This would take them through the most important part of their development and into senior ranks. This is what I did with the group that came through more specifically to train with me. This is the group that for six months I took to all of the training camps increasing their weekly randoris to 50+.

I was travelling all over Belgium identifying talent to bring in to my group. Invitations were given to them to come to daily training and to the weekly randoris. After six months of intensive change it was clear who was going to stay with the program and who was not. We helped with the development of the group but also with the coaches at the centre and in the clubs. I was also working closely with sports science, Paul Ponnet, with physio, Tomverhoeven and with the doctor, Peter Smolders who made up our support team. They became firm friends throughout my stay in Belgium. I built up a strong base of fighters who remained faithful and to this day stay in touch with me and visit me on a regular basis.

It was where I also learned a lot about working with Federations and funding bodies, more so than in Wales, as Niki and Keven had dealt with that mostly. I couldn't blame the BJA now for not understanding me, and the way I worked, as this wasn't the BJA, nor was it Britain. I was soon to find out that it was an epidemic that affects a lot of countries, especially the smaller nations.

The Performance Director had her work cut out for her from the onset of her job, as she was only 26 years of age. She had to line manage three, forty/fifty -something year old male coaches who had more years in coaching than she had on the earth. It couldn't have been easy. I later found out that this was the tactic of the funding body: Get them in young so they could control them.

How could you have an educated opinion based on experience at such a young age? You just want a job, or more so a career, and to do it properly and well enough that they will recommend you to the next step.

She was also caught in middle between myself and these meddlesome personal coaches. Their athletes didn't want to be part of my system. They were too used to ruling the roost and wanted to do it their way. Well I had seen that before in '96 and knew it didn't work, but I only wanted athletes who wanted to work with me. Anything other than cooperation was a detriment to the system and the cohesion we, as a team had created. It unfortunately made an 'us and them' scenario which was far from ideal, however I felt I was there to develop the team, not just one player. I have to say, I didn't stop trying to get them on board, athlete and coach, but my attempts were futile.

These athletes were able to go directly to the funding body, skirting the whole system put in place, giving them immunity from any Federation obligations. It must have been tough to monitor two sets of rules and me not understanding that (or not wanting to) must have made it even more difficult. It was getting to the point now that every decision I made seemed to be either ignored, undermined or overturned. I was just a baby sitter in the end, pushing paper. It wasn't what I signed up for, nor did I see how I could make a difference with such constraints. It became more than the money at that point. I had a clear head now and had stopped playing the victim or 'woe is me'. Time to take hold of my own destiny and finally be my own boss.

I was there for 3 ½ years and on reflection it was a happy time, a busy time, but pleasant enough, especially once I stopped the drinking. In truth, I probably didn't get to see and experience much of the country as Niki and the girls did, as I was travelling so much and was never really 'home'. And that was the case really that helped make the next decision of my life path. What was 'home'? I missed the UK and the thought of living the next part of our life together there kept calling to me.

Niki and I thought carefully about our return to the UK and where we would live. France was on the cards at one point. Staying in Belgium but maybe down to the Ardennes, where Niki preferred? The girls wanted to stay, of course, because they had made such great friends and didn't want to leave that and thinking about it, they really did spend what were their formative years there. Losing the pool and large garden wasn't a great selling point either.

So we made a list of what we wanted and needed for our new home. We were in a good spot financially speaking for the first time in a long time, as we had finally rented out the house for the 3 years we had been away to cover the mortgage and were very diligent in our spending and saving in Belgium.

So our plan had worked. It had been a lonely, exhausting way of doing it, however a lot of good came from it.

Looking at our list, we wanted:
- a project to renovate
- and it would need to be near an airport
- Good schools are always a factor
- And Niki wanted a real sense of community, which she had missed while in Belgium

She did make a couple of lovely friends who we still visit and keep in contact with now, but in Belgium, it seemed that people keep themselves to themselves, which for me is fine, but for someone as sociable as Niki, it had been a lonely time.

Again, she was in a foreign country, not knowing anyone, no parental support to help with the girls, and while I was away, spending her time alone in the house, pushing to get the NAEF business off the ground, ready to hit the ground running, wherever that ground might end up being.

It became clear one day while I was away with the team and a call came through from Niki.

'You'll never guess where I am standing, Neil.'

'No you're right. I can't. I can't even remember where I am at the moment.' And this was the case many times. I had to keep looking at my boarding pass most times to remind myself what country I was going to and what the date was.

'I'm standing in the courtyard at Furze Barns.'

This in itself was surprising. I knew she was going back to the UK but just to visit friends in Yelvertoft. She hated that house now. She didn't ever want to go there, let alone on her own.

'Is Jenny with you?'

'Nope. Just me,' she quipped.

'Why are you there?'

'Well Jenny and I got to talking. Ok, mostly drinking, but also discussing what you and I should do next. I told her our checklist and she just looked at me and said, 'Don't you already have a house to fix up, with good motor links, near the airport and great schools?' I have to say it did get me thinking.'

'And?'

'Well, I can see it again. I can see our vision for this place. I think maybe that's why I called off the bailiffs. Maybe, I guess. Oh I don't know. It's a thought though, no?'

'And the neighbours?'

We had a massive falling out with one of the neighbours over land purchase, access and boundaries that lasted most of our time there before moving to Wales. It was the main reason Niki didn't want to be there.

'Well, new news there, as well. Seems we were the common enemy, amongst other things, I guess, and as soon as we were out of the picture, things didn't go too well over there. They've split up and he's come over to me to apologise for everything. It was all very overwhelming, really. Like a black cloud has been blown away from over the Barns. I wish you were here to feel it. It's different somehow. I think this might be the way forward, Neil.'

And forward it was. I came home from the event and we started the plans for our return to the UK, however with a different mind-set and a different perception. It was going to be tough as our income was going to be cut in half. However, the control over our lives was going to triple. Oh, there was going to be stress, but at least it wasn't someone else's stress just passed onto us.

Our platform was to be an international Judo company based in Britain, not a British Judo company. This was always going to be difficult to pull off as I was such an iconic part of the British Judo scene in the 80s that people still just assume that I am with the British Judo Association. Working with the VJF and Belgium has helped that to a degree but only really at the elite, competitive level. I had a year of people asking, 'Where have you been?'

To the masses, our target audience, I was still *Mr.* British Judo and in their eyes, only an elite coach. It was going to be difficult to find and cultivate the independence and the world-wide recognition as the brand: *Neil Adams.* The fight now was to demonstrate to Judoka around the world that I have the skills to develop grassroots as well as elite performance.

I had always fought to be different, not to be part of the pack, to make my mark and stand out. I had to stop and think, and a few very important questions started to bubble to the surface, ones that I most likely should have asked myself years ago:

When did that stop? That drive, to be different.
When did I, *me*, defeat me?
Why did that stop?
Why did I let that happen?
How did I let them, others, do that?

It's been progressive, but I've come to realise that I let people take that drive away from me in order to further themselves. The failure of the Olympics, the ending of my first marriage, the temporary loss of my relationship with my son, the untimely death of my brother didn't help the fact, either. But, I let in the belief that I was now part of the pack, or worse, behind it. It saddens me that people wanted me to believe this so then I wasn't a threat, instead of making me one of their biggest assets.

In retrospect I see this started way back in 1988, when my job of winning medals was done and suddenly I was competition for the coaching positions. And as I didn't end on a high note at Olympics, there were cracks in the armour. The seeds of doubt were planted, watered by the '96 catastrophe and nurtured by the ostracising by the BJA in 2001.

As with everything, hindsight is 20/20 and we can see why certain things have happened and the lessons we have had to learn to get to where we need to be. It seems to me, the harder we fight against these lessons, the Universe just pushes back even harder until we 'get it'.

Well, I can't say I 'get' all of it, but I've been able to reflect and understand it to a degree, enough to move past it and build myself up again. One quote that resounds with me and probably will until my next lessons are learned is:

I will forgive, but I won't forget.

Neil, reflecting

14. The Big Question and The Hard Answer

In 2012, I had reached a point in my life that I wanted to leave a legacy.

It wasn't going to be in creating an Olympic Champion, be it myself, or someone else. That just wasn't going to happen anymore, and I had to let that go.

With that out of the way, my real passion emerged. I realised I could really make a difference to the sport overall. I knew I had skills and experience to give and why give it to one country at a time? Why not be available to the sport as a whole?

I then clicked in to Niki's vision of coach education and saw what she saw while working away in Sint Job. It's not just about the athletes, really. They are only going to do what the coaches tell them to do. If we are going to make a difference in the sport, a real difference, globally, we need to invest in our coaches and ensure that these coaches, especially from grassroots up to elite, realise their acute responsibility in being technically skilled and be continually up-skilled to create an unshakable foundation.

It needs to be based on traditional skills and concepts, ones we know work, and for all of us to become insanely proficient at these, so as to then adapt and form variations to suit individuals and categories.

I really believe this is the only way our sport will not only sustain itself, but survive. I'm all for evolution and new things, however we can never lose sight of the foundation and must return periodically to review, re-test, and re-evaluate the paths.

This is all about legacy and leaving something that can be passed on to generations of future Judoka that will help them in their quest for technical excellence. This is how Olympic champions are made. OK that… and a wee bit of that luck from Cinderella's Fairy Godmother doesn't hurt either.

When I reflect on some of the stories in this book it has been a mixture of sadness, frustration, in some cases disbelief, but there has also been lots of happiness and laughter and lots of lessons learned. We all need to learn from our lessons in life and there are probably many of you out there that believe in fate. I am now a big believer in creating our own destiny and making things happen.

So, when did that stop? When was it that I lost my direction, to be different?

I think I gave in to the notion of believing everyone thought of me as second. No matter what I did to be on top of something, there was always someone there trying to knock me down or take it away from me.

I think if I had been completely sober throughout these times, that drive would have been there. The clarity I needed to fight back at them, make the right decisions and to take the right course of action. However, in trying to cope with my own disappointment from as far back as losing the Olympics, I used alcohol to dull that feeling of 'woe is me'.

The disappointment I felt for myself, and the disappointment of me I knew must be in others. Of course this was my own perception, but if I felt like this, surely others must do. I knew Alison did, as she kept saying to me, 'Where is your drive? You just don't have it anymore.' I know now that she was most likely coming from a place of concern, and love. However, I took it as an affirmation of what people thought of me, of what she thought of me. It didn't take much to believe it as truth.

Some of you may be shocked at how honestly I talk about this. I have people say to me, 'but you've never been a drinker,' when I tell them. The truth is that a lot of people who drink too much can operate at a high functioning level. They can cover it up most of the time and for a while that's good enough. But never, ever for long. So I hope reading about what happened to me helps some people. Especially those who might have a drinking problem and like to pretend that they have it under control. I know all the excuses:

'I only have a couple of beers…

A glass of wine for pleasure,

I can stop whenever I want'.

It is a problem that can escalate over a period of time and many don't see it coming. They think there's nothing wrong and they think that the only person they hurt is themselves. Like smokers who claim passive smoking isn't their problem.

In my clarity, that now makes me angry. Because it's NEVER just you. People that drink or take drugs for whatever reasons might think that it is all about them but the truth of the matter is that it is family and friends and everyone around them that are affected by it and that's the devastation, it's not just you. I know, and so does my son.

My drinking really affected him, I didn't realise how much, in the early days. I had a very special relationship with him, I spent a lot of time with him and a lot of it was quality time. He had this dad that still trained, and trained hard, but in the end was compensating more training for more drinks. I took on another kind of personality when I had a drink or two and in the end he started to notice.

As I've said before, I was not aggressive or physical in any way, I was spacey, forgetful, not really in the game. He really objected to that and he felt really deeply that he wanted to do something about it, but he didn't know what to do and nor did the people closest to me. He was a lost soul when I look back and we've had discussions about it since. He's 30 years of age this year. We have a great relationship now and he's proud it went the way it has. But it was so hard on him.

Especially when I got the DUI. I'd split with Alison and was living with Niki in the bedsit. Ashley was only 14 at the time and his mother was late back from the Prison where she worked. He heard noises outside and thought someone was trying to get into the house. He got scared, because he had been woken up by the noise and found he was still alone. So Ashley called me and said there were people trying to get and his mum wasn't home from work yet. So I went tearing over there. Up in a flash, out of bed, and into the car. It was only a mile down the road, but… I'd just had a glass of wine before getting onto bed.

And I got pulled over.

And lost my license.

This was a real dilemma, as Niki had just moved over and hadn't yet learned to drive on this side of the road. Our livelihood and getting Ashley to and from school depended on her learning, and learning quickly. It was definite baptism by fire. It should have been a sign then.

This brings me to my definition of an alcoholic.

Am I an alcoholic?

At the risk of sounding condescending and I, in no way, mean to, I believe I am not. I was able to stop too easily and found that I was not dependent on it to get me through the day. At one point I thought so, as I suffered terribly from panic attacks.

These panic attacks were crippling. I was very good at hiding them, but it did affect my life enormously. I had one or two incidents where it could have been quite evident. The one thing that made it evident was I had trouble signing my name for autographs at seminars and public appearances. It got to the stage that I would buy notebooks and fill them with signatures in private, so I could just pass them out when out in public. I didn't want to be caught out.

I was, caught out, a couple of times, however. A teenage lad asked me to sign a piece paper and I had no pages left. I had no choice but to try and sign it without looking like an idiot. Just the thought of it made me break out in a sweat. I struggled through it and it looked nothing like the others pages I had just handed out. The boy looked at it, realised it wasn't the same as the others and asked me to do it again. I looked at him trying to ascertain whether it was out of pure devilment, seeing me struggle, or if he really did want one just like all the others.

Such was my mind set. Everyone was out to get me. Everyone wanted to put me down. Having a sneaky drink calmed my nerves. Well it does, doesn't it? Just have a nip to 'take the edge off'. We all do it. We are all taught to do it. It's ok then to have a drink to help cope as it works, right? Sure it does, but not when you are in a cycle. My cycle, and it's different for everyone, was:

a) having a drink to forget my pain,

b) panic attack when out of that fuzz, scared that people would find out 'my little secret',

c) have a drink to calm the panic attack and get back into that comfort zone again.

The other time was at the bank. We had to ask for a loan to get the down payment on the mortgage for Furze Barns. Niki signed her place and passed it over to me to sign in my place. The world went into slow motion. What felt like an eternity must have only been a minute, but enough time for Niki and the bank manager to look at me with concern.

'Neil, are you ok?' Niki touched my arm.

'I, ah, just need a minute.' And I got up out of the chair and walked out of the office and out of the bank into the fresh air.

I knew I looked like death warmed over, I could feel the clammy, cold sweat all over my body. I had to get back in there and do this. If I couldn't sign my name, we wouldn't have a house. The pressure of this one simple task was immense.

I walked back into the bank and into the manager's office. I sat down ignoring the frightened look from Niki and the slightly concerned one from the manager. I pulled the paper towards me and what must have looked like a toddler scratching their name, I signed the paper. I fell back into the chair and looked at Niki,

'Can we go now?'

I've never been a good liar. Niki always jokes that 'MI6 will not be calling.' I thought I was, as I took to hiding my 'medicine' in stashes all around the place. That, or it was easy enough to get at the shop and throw it into a Fanta bottle, my mixer of choice. So I was never far from it. It's too easy in our culture, here in Britain and I would hazard a guess in Europe in general as it is such an accepted way of recreation and so very accessible.

Pam, my mother in law, created an intervention one time while we lived in Wales. Niki had finally reached out for some help. Pam asked her why we still had alcohol in the house, and we did. We had a well stocked bar. Well stocked because I never touched it. That would be an instant give away! Niki told her mum that it would be a futile exercise as it is so easy to get alcohol. She couldn't be with me every second of the day.

And this is the thing! It is so a part of our British culture that we don't even think about it until it's too late or we have an event/scare. It's something we have seen our parents and adults throughout our childhood do and it is learned behaviour. How could it not? It is only since I stopped drinking that I realised just how easy it was to acquire an alcoholic drink versus a non-alcoholic one at any given function. Even today I attend functions for the IJF or top class events and all the wine and champagne you can take for free, but I have to go and buy my Coca Cola! I often have to bring a bottle of soft drink to BBQs to ensure I'm not on tap water all night, as it's not thought that someone would not be drinking a beer or wine, or both.

Why did I stop drinking, or rather what made me stop

drinking? It was the event in Belgium as I said. I think that it was actually seeing the disappointed looks of people and not just imagining them any more. I think it was the realisation that 'hey, I'm better than this! I have skills. I have everything going for me. Who are you to look at me like that?!'

And with that, I woke up.

I am *Neil Adams*, World Champion, multiple Olympic medallist, father, husband, son and friend. I am good at it. I am really good at it. What I have now makes me very happy and the things I don't have and want, I have the skills to go and get.

Then a piece of memory floated back into my mind Niki's face of complete imploring, but calmness for I think she had finally come to the end of trying everything. She said, 'If you're not going to do it for you or for me, please do it for our girls. They are young enough to not remember any of this and I don't want the way they look at you now to ever change.'

I remember saying in a defensive outburst, 'I would die for them! You know that!'

She looked straight at me and with a mother bear stare and stated, ' Yes, but I want you to live for them, Neil.'

I then saw my best friend, Chris Bowles' face, float into view hearing him talk to Niki, saying that it was worse than she wanted to admit, that he was there to help in any way but what I really needed from him was a good heart to heart, and a mirror.

Some people call it an A-HA! moment. That's what it was; all done in a flash, me sitting in that solitary chair, surrounded by people shaking their heads.

Well I was done with the head-shaking people. I was done with the disappointment. I had wasted too much time thinking of what could've been and not enough of what I have and how to take it further. I wasn't about to let my legacy be about being washed up and hung out to dry.

I had to finally ask myself, 'What am I doing this for?'

Why am I chancing my incredible relationship that I have with Niki, my incredible relationship that I have with my son and two beautiful girls, they look on me with awe and it is wonderful, why, why chance that?

For what?

You know I couldn't even think of a proper reason really other than all of the things that had happened in the past. The way the BJA treated me, the near misses in my competitive career, the bankruptcy and of course losing Chris my brother. All of that was horrific, all of that had hurt me.

None of it was worth chancing the things in my life I adored.

If I could ask you take away anything from this book, it's this: Perseverance. We are still learning. We need to always re-adjust. I think it's as simple as asking ourselves, every time, 'Is this a problem?'

If it is a problem, then what do we do to fix it?

How do we re-adjust the factors to solve it or learn from it?

Do we need more skills or help to enable us to solve it?
Is it our problem in the first place?

If it's not then, let it go.

I know, I know. Easier said than done. However, know this: if you, yourself cannot change the factors within that problem or situation, then you need to let it go, as no matter what you try to do, it will not change it. It is not yours to change. The only thing you can control is how you react to it, how you cope with it, whether you enable the behaviour, person, situation or not. Take what you can from it and then send it on its way. It is the secret to sanity. And by that, I mean being a whole person, true to yourself, and not only for you, but for your family and your friends. If you are coach, it is for the athletes and in business, your co-workers. It's an ever-working process and I think it's meant to be.

Not the most flattering imagery, but I was once in the men's room at Bath University. I was presenting one of the practical sessions. I was using the cubicle, for the obvious reasons, and heard two men walk in. It was Simon Hicks from Fighting Films and Roy Inman, who was an instructor there at Bath.

Oblivious to me being there, they were talking pleasantries and then there was the obligatory pause in proceedings. The talk turned to British Judo, and all that it entailed, at the sink, and then I heard Roy as he opened the door to leave.

'You know what's wrong with Neil Adams?... '

I never heard the answer. The door had shut closed, proverbially and materially. I sat there, mind motoring,
'What?! What is wrong with Neil Adams?!' my mind screamed.

There were two ways to handle this. Go up to Roy and ask what he meant by the comment. But that would be confrontational and would I get the true answer? Not likely. The other was to try and forget it happened. Well we can see that worked well, didn't it. Here I am writing about it.

I never did find out what the end of Roy and Simon's conversation, as sadly both have passed now. My point here is that if I heard the end, what was I prepared to do about it? Or maybe this was just one of those wonderful things the Universe does to make you work for it and search out and work out that lesson on your own. I do hope, however, that I've since stuffed their answer right up the proverbial!

Neil accepting his induction into the IJF Hall of Fame

15. A Legacy of Education

Let's talk about Legacy. I think I've been a bit apprehensive to think about leaving a legacy as I equate it to the 'end', and I'm not good on the subject of death. Never have been. I have been forced to face it though, as of late, as many of my friends have left us due to one form of Cancer or another, and the tragic death of my brother, Chris which I will speak about later on. It has forced me to look at it and with the clarity I now have without 'taking the edge off' the situation and pushing it down with a hidden refreshment.

I want to be known for continually *developing* my legacy, not known just for it. Not yet anyway.

And a lot of people do ask me, 'what now?' I say to them it's not finished yet. This next chapter is still to be written and there still many things that I want to achieve in life. I said to Niki at one stage in our lives it would be nice not to have to worry about money and where the next month's mortgage payment is coming from. From a business point of view I have been naïve beyond belief, but I endeavour to get better and to learn from my mistakes.

I have put most of my legacy focus on the skills that I can give to the Judo community. Those traditional, fundamental skills that I see deteriorating while on my travels on the World Judo Tour. There are some amazing fighting skills from the top fighters, but to me it is only a solid few, and I would like to see many, many more championing for any given title.

Maybe deteriorating is the wrong word. Maybe a lack of focus is a better way to describe it. We always knew that we wanted to get a resource out on these fundamental skills. The first obstacle was having the right technology to get them out there. We had some false starts, but the technology and the audience culture has caught up, with what we wanted to do, ultimately. We knew it had to be in video, it was just how to get it out to everyone. The Youtube culture hasn't helped us in that way as there is a lot of videos out there for free that I believe are incorrect technique, if not down right dangerous to body and mind. Let's face it, it's true, you get what you pay for.

Learning Judo is like learning a language. You need the basic grammar, and the building blocks, before you can have a conversation. That's what great coaches and trainers do. They're teachers and, like all teachers, they and their pupils do their best work when they're able to tailor that work to individuals.

If I teach you a technique, my job as a trainer is to get you to be able to achieve that. What happens a lot now in coach education is we have a lot of tick box situations, that's what's wrong with online university stuff actually a lot of the time – there's no assessment afterwards. In other words you can learn something from a book, you can learn how to write down the answers and you can get the right answers but if you can't put that in a teaching context that's not a good thing. And if you can't put that in a teaching context when you're training international athletes, then you're doing them, their country and yourself a crucial disservice.

Niki and I talk about it a lot. Some of these kids, great athletes, great potential but sometimes they don't learn how to play the game well enough. They have no adaptability. Every sport has a game. Every sport has rules. How you play that game can be the difference between winning and losing. One of the most important things I do if I've got a class who know nothing about Judo is I tell them how they can win at our game. If you don't tell them how to win it's like putting a football down in front of 22 players and saying 'off you go' and they have a kick around. You need to explain the goals, the offside rule and get them thinking from a tactical point of view. So learning the game is very important.

I think also being tactically aware about what you're up against, having done your homework is very important. I was talking to a couple of athletes recently about knowing the game and how to win. One of them was talking about the new rules and complaining there were certain things about the rules that could be interpreted in certain ways, depending on the referee. Many people talk about interpretation but remember the referees are only interpreting to their level. I think that this is why there is so much variation when it comes to interpretation in our sport. They hadn't thought about how they could be interpreted, had never thought about how the referee might interpret those rules and did not have a game plan. They never thought of studying the referee as well as their opponent.

I said 'that's not good enough, you're in the top ten in the world and that's not good enough. You have to do your homework and if you're not willing to put the work in and go in there fully prepared, then prepare to fail. It's not just the physical preparation, it's not just the mental preparation, it's not just being skilful enough to win at that level, it is *knowing* the game, knowing how to play the game and being prepared.

My dad always said technical excellence was most important. Everything we did was geared towards technical training – I only had two major individual competitions a year, the Area and the British Championships. All of the other competitions we did were team competitions, so the problem now I feel is that a lot of the junior clubs gauge their success by the amount of medals the kids win, not necessarily what the kids are doing to achieve their aims. For many, for the coaches to be recognised as a great coach it's about: 'this is how many medals I've produced from these kids'. I really don't believe that's the way it should be, I think that technical development in the early stages is the most important thing, it put me in good stead and my father laid that foundation.

I think that if you focus on results you will never change. If you focus on change then the results will come.

My mum and dad backed me a million per cent and for that I am so grateful. It was what I wanted to do but not necessarily what was best in some ways. I think that finishing my school education at 16 was not necessarily the best thing to do. It is now at least 18 years old before you finish school and you now have a better chance of higher education afterwards.

Does this matter when you've got this fantastic life travelling here, there and everywhere? No, not in the early years, but it certainly becomes more important when you're coming to the end of your career. The change from being an active athlete at the top of your field to being out in the big wide world and having to make a living can be very sudden.

Niki has two degrees and for me she's proof it can be done although in order to compete at the highest level you have to get a balance between the educational needs and training. Judo athletes have an intelligence to play our game, but those with the right mental application can go all the way. But it's no good if you're concentrating so hard on the academia to the point where the physical training can only be done to a certain point, but if there's the right balance, it can be done. And we need both mental and physical stimulation.

The thing is, we cannot leave it up to the athletes as to what they think they should do. Good coaching is guiding them when required and telling them what they should be doing because more often than not, they don't know what they want or how to get there. That's why coach education is so important to us.

This is one reason we have turned our focus to coach education. So much that is going wrong in coach education, internationally, being that there's not enough technical base being introduced at an early level. There is too much emphasis on competition results and of course we're losing the kids early, they're having early burn out. This is what we have to address.

It's really important that we avoid the early burn out and prepare them right for the job at hand. The coaches need to know how to guide and how to do it in the right way. There is a process and a lot of them are too busy concentrating on their small ponds and small pools and don't really see the big picture.

That's the advantage time has given me. Starting out I had one direction, which was the physical, the Judo one, to become the best. Was it going to make me a million pounds? I didn't think of that at the time, I just wanted the success and then I was going to think about the other bit.

The journalistic bit has come later, and that's a nice direction, if not a Godsend. What I started to do quite early on, was the coaching side of it, I realised I wanted to pass things on coaching-wise and it always seems like a natural progression from competitor to coach. I remember the first coaching lessons I taught were very technical but only my particular technique and only what I did:

'This is what I do and I do it well so I want to show you how good I am at it!'

That worked well and people would invite me for a time and I would show them my special move and then I realised it was much broader than that. I realised that I just showed them everything, why would they ask me back? I needed repeat business, so I started to break it down and left them wanting me back for more. So I started to ask myself what was needed on these courses? If I show a technique to someone, do they understand it? As a coach I needed to understand how to teach it and how to break it down and if I want you to be a coach, I need to be able to deliver it so you can replicate it to your class.

That's how I developed over the last 20 years, this is how I developed my coaching. A lot of the things I introduce first as a concept. Things like balance, direction, movement, adaptability, and being a good partner or *Uke*. My job is to get you to understand it and then to deliver it. For me that is the secret of the longevity of Judo, that's what's going to help the skill levels to rise and then maintain.

I have noticed that a lot of coaching courses that are available at the moment, are advertised as very much 'tick box' coaching. As long as you tick all the boxes you get a certificate and then you can coach. The question is though now you 'know' it but can you 'do' it?

So my thoughts were that we need to make people accountable and we need to assess how you deliver it and deliver it in a certain way, that I know works. A lot of the things that I've done with the kids and adults is to develop skills, and how to pass those skills on and I think that is the way to go.

We wanted to teach people how to do it correctly so as to have a strong base, *then* start playing with it to adapt it best to their own abilities. To me, the Gokyo is as traditional as you can get and a starting block that Judoka all over the world know and recognise.

The Gokyo comprises of 40 fundamental throwing techniques. It is divided into sets of progressive skills awarded with a different coloured belt for each set:
Yellow,
Orange,
Green,
Blue and
Brown.

It was the obvious starting point. Researching what was out there, we saw that it was all demonstration with no close ups or real study - in layman terms, rather than sports science jargon, which is always a danger - of each of the important reference points or teaching points that can be easily replicated and passed on to the next generation. Which leads me to the next obstacle we encountered.

The Black Belt is both a blessing and a curse. I am not going to go into my argument about grades and the grading process as that would be a whole other chapter, if not book, but what I will say is that I believe the belt is an indication of skill and ability to do that skill, end of argument. I am an 8th Dan and I am still seeking out ways to do things differently. I am on the continual hunt on how to improve either my own skills base or, in my position as Sensei, those of my students. I do not look to the years I have put in to the sport to dictate what grade I should be.

I want to be able to demonstrate my physical skill and technical knowledge of Judo at any given time, to whomever may ask it of me. If it was up to me, I would have us all go back to our competitive grades as that truly illustrates a holistic knowledge of physical, tactical and technical skills. I know different countries have different syllabi and grading criteria and that many have opted to take the fighting element out so as to accommodate those who are injured or dislike the competition side of things. However, I believe this is not being true to the Art or the Sport.

Everything in Judo is based on a circle, so the knowledge wheel must be as well. I wouldn't like to be in a school where the teachers only know half of their subject. I wouldn't want to go into brain surgery where the surgeon has only studied it in theory and was not that great or disliked the physical aspect of it. To be fair, I don't think either would get very far in their elected fields.

If Judokas are serious about keeping the Sport and the Art, not only alive, but thriving, we need to all take responsibility in fortifying our skills base and foundations and seriously take on the responsibility of up-skilling and assessing our own skills.

It does not stop at the Black Belt. The Black Belt means you have completed the foundation elements and that should mean to a high standard. It also means your continual studies must now turn to how to teach those skills, maintaining that high standard set by obtaining your own and continuing the quest for knowledge.

We don't know everything. We can't know everything. Besides, what fun would that be? I suspect this is a common thread in other sports, and careers, as Judo can, and is often used as a metaphor for life with Kano's, the founder of Judo's philosophy of: *Maximum Efficiency, Minimum Effort*. This, however does not come without work. Those who make it look easy have had many a hard hour to make it so.

It is with these philosophies, Kano's and mine, that we developed *Judo Excellence*. It is an online resource that we hope will stand the test of time as the techniques have already been around for more than 100 years. It is meant as a tool for students and coaches to learn, review, adapt. It is the flagship of my Legacy project.

Having our daughters start into the sport has been a wake up call as well. Not only in terms of suddenly having more sympathy as a parent of a child in sport. Though, I have already had that as Ashley has always been a keen sportsman, mostly in Rugby Union, but a natural in most sports he puts his hand to.

But now I found myself suddenly from an all men's team to an all women's team, as Niki is also a former Olympian, as was stated earlier, for the Canadian Olympic Judo Team in 1996. Using our girls as guinea pigs, one might say, we have developed training aids to help in the coaching and training process.

We studied how best to approach the girls' training in terms of getting the body ready for technique and full on Judo movement. Niki and I thought hard about what worked best for both of us and also thought what we would have liked to have had when we were training.

Just as an aside, my former training partner, Ray Stevens,

couldn't believe the Nage Komi Wall mat we designed. He just stared at me, wide eyed, and said,

'Where was that when we were training? That would have saved my back a lot of trouble!'

And gratefully we do hear that a lot now. We have the uchi komi (resistance) bands that are progressive in their resistance so Judokas can work up to their goals of 180 degree turn-ins, and use them for rehabilitation to work back to where they were before injury. They are also an amazing fitness tool and I use them on my travels where there is no gym, or even as a break from the rower just for something different. They are so mobile. I just throw them in my bag.

We have developed a Balance Mat, as I believe that beginners should learn the concepts first before technique. Concepts such as: Movement, Direction, Balance, Communication & Cooperation, Kuzushi (Breaking Balance), Ukemi (Falling Safely), and Adaptability. If you give them these, then when you move onto technique, the body and the mind have their own AHA! Moments.

I must stress here that beginners and children, to me, are not to be used interchangeably. I think a lot of clubs and Federations get this incorrect. Beginners are those starting in the sport, be they 7, 27, 37, 47 years of age, so not necessarily children. The application or presentation to these different age groups will be different, but they all have to learn the same concepts and skills.

We all learn by our senses and up until now learning the different concepts and moves for a Judo technique has only been by feel, or by trial and error. There are all the ways of learning and a lot of thought is going into this institution of thought of which I am a firm student. We have developed the Balance Mat so as to tie in sight and feel. The student not only feels where they need to be, but has a reference point on the mat to study to and replicate. In all our equipment we strive for improved and proper muscle memory training because our sport is so heavily based on repetition. We might as well use our time wisely and effectively and aim for as close to perfection each time. Many will have heard me use the quote, 'Practice does not make perfect, it makes Permanent.' This is the ethos to all my training, past and present.

***

The Voice of Judo. I must admit, I am proud of that name as this has also been years in the making, but one that has come relatively easy to me. Listening to my videos where I started with Fighting Films, I am glad my voice has dropped and I no longer sound like a young David Beckham. No, no… no need to go searching for the tapes, take my word for it.

Fighting Films really was (and is) a great platform for me. It has kept my name in the forefront for many years, even though now people know my voice rather than my face. I owe them a lot, as it helped me to lay a foundation. I've had the pleasure of working with Simon Hicks who we've sadly lost to Cancer. However, his son, Danny has taken over and is doing an unprecedented and amazing job with the business, along with Simon's widow, Sharron and I know Simon would be extremely proud of both of them on how far they have taken it all.

It has only been later in my career, that broadcasting has become a big part of my life. To commentate and announce at the 2012 London Olympic Games was a great honour, and it is something that I enjoy tremendously. I am enthusiastic with my commentary, and from the impersonations I get from time to time, I guess it shows through. That's the way I am. I'm enthusiastic, passionate and I have a true love for my sport.

It is developing well. At first we struggled with the planning and structure of the business. Successful business people surround themselves with good people and get experts in for the bits they don't know or can't do themselves. That's what we try to do, I'm not afraid to surround myself with competent people. We just need to keep on pushing forwards.

Niki and I teamed up for the Commonwealth Games commentary in 2014 in Glasgow, and she's great at that too. She has a unique way of expressing herself and that makes her very special in so many ways.

In fact, it was hilarious. We were good cop, bad cop. I was trying to stay really calm and technical and she was the one coming out with all the funnies. Of course they want her back, hopefully for more Olympic or Commonwealth Games. It was a great platform for us at the Commonwealth Games in Glasgow because we had so many British athletes who were in the medals, so we got lots of airtime... She was funny, she'd say things she should never have said on air! I'd say 'you can't say that, we're live!' and that's what people remember of course. That's entertainment.

I haven't commentated at the Olympics for a while but will be commentating at the 2016 Olympics in Rio De Janeiro. At the last Olympics in London I was asked to announce at the Olympic Judo event. It was my first announcing job actually, and what a place to start!

I wouldn't have thought I was the first choice as there are many great announcers out there but they wanted an English announcer, and someone to double the commentary who knew what they were talking about, so they asked me if I'd do it. And of course I went for it! I did it, and I'm proud to have done it. It was a great experience and one that I will never forget.

It's fun, but also it's a tough thing to do. You're live, you're struggling with some really difficult names and this is one of the most important days of these athlete's lives. I try to get the names right and at speed it is sometimes difficult but it is about taking your time and often looking at the word phonetically and breaking it into sections. In commentary you can cheat by calling them 'The' Georgian or 'The' Russian but with announcing you have to be more exact.

You've got to announce their names and if you're doing a medal presentation, you can't mess that up. You're announcing the Olympic Gold medallist, the Olympic medallists, the people presenting the flowers and you cannot mess them up.

One time in London, the name was so long that it didn't fit on the scoreboard. This was often my fail safe when announcing. In the end I had to cut it up phonetically on paper and I just about got it out, nobody complained, thank goodness, so it must have been alright.

Another time they put a piece of paper in front of me:

'No pressure or *anything Neil*, but just to your left, Mr. Vladimir Putin is just walking in with the Prime Minister and the Duke and Duchess of York, don't mess it up. Oh and the Duke of Edinburgh is due to arrive, we just don't know when, so stand by…'

This is in between announcing the fights and in-house commentary. I thought 'oh boy… can't mess this up,' again the pressure was on. The dandy of them all was when I had to announce the North Korean onto the mat. This was a delicate situation, because just recently a South Korean flag been put up at one of the events instead of the North Korean flag. A massive, political mistake. It was all over the papers so my director said 'whatever you do you can't mix up North/South Korea. It's People's Republic of Korea and its South Korea'. So looking down my draw list I have got one fighter, People's Republic of China and underneath Korea.

When I was announcing all I saw was Peoples Republic of and Korean underneath it and so I announced it as Peoples Republic of Korea for a South Korean and I thought, I'm dead, this is it, and I'm finished.

Nobody noticed or came up to me.

It was one of my ex full time students who came up to me about a day later and asked 'did you mess the Korean name up?' and I clapped him over the mouth and said 'you can't say anything! It never happened' I could feel his smirk underneath my hand but he kept quiet luckily. Nobody said a thing and I live to tell the tale.

Neil takes 2nd place on the podium

16. Lessons in Losing

I hate losing, I don't like the feelings it gives me, but I'm a lot better now at explaining it and explaining the experience of losing. The first piece of good advice I was given was in 1978 when I lost for the first time in a real competition. It was this:

Smile.

Because people always, always notice when you don't smile. So the smiling bit was massive, even in loss. Then come off, get out of the sight of the public, and then kick the chairs or whatever you do but remember to smile.

Even then, be careful. At the 1980 Olympic Games where I lost on a split decision and an ITV pundit called Gary Newbon, keen as mustard at the time and young, came up to me directly after my Olympic final loss and shoved a mic right under my nose with his words of 'how do you feel?' I wanted to say 'how I feel right now, right this very second, Gary is like shoving that microphone from where it will have to be surgically removed,' but the fact is you have to take it, you have to learn to do that.

That's what we don't do at the moment, train our athletes on how to handle media. It should be part of an athlete's education. They need it and it can make a difference financially to them as well. If people see a happy persona and a positive one, then they're much more likely to get sponsorship deals. If they see a miserable, bad tempered person, then they're just not going to be interested. Or you'll get the wrong interest and get branded, and remember that shit sticks!

Journalists also have a responsibility to be sensitive to the situation too. You're talking to an athlete who's just lost on one of the most important days of their lives so you have to be gentle. You say, 'did it go according to your game plan? No? What went wrong?' And work your way around it that way. To say to someone that's just lost a World Title, European Title, Olympic Title, 'how do you feel?'

Listen, you know how they feel.

Or at least you have some sort of empathetic inkling as to how they feel. Their world has just dropped out from beneath them and they feel devastated, so we don't really need to ask that. Let's ask interesting things. We need to know the positive things really, what went right or what went wrong in that particular match, how are you going to put it right the next time, when are you training? It's got to be positive. It was 1980, 36 years ago and I still remember the first thing that came out of his mouth.

That's why we spend so much time teaching kids to get positives from both victory and defeat. Learn, all the time. Because it will only ever make you a better Judoka and human being.

I'm taking you back again, back to 1976 when I remember getting a silver medal in the British Open. I was competing as a junior fighter in the Seniors with a chance of winning a selection for the Montreal Olympic Games. I lost a very close final to Vas Morrison who won the place but at such a young age I was first reserve for the greatest event on Earth.

I remember giving an interview afterwards and I was a bit disrespectful, I think, to Vas. And Vas was a great Judoka who went to the Olympic Games. He fought for 3rd place and he didn't lose by a lot. I was a bit disrespectful and I apologised to him afterwards. I said 'Hey, I was disrespectful there and I didn't mean to, really. I was being a bit of an ass,' and that youthful arrogance was something I had to change. It was something I had to get a hold of and get control of.

One of the things I've pushed all the way through my

career is how important it is to bounce back and that was a lesson I began learning when I lost to Vas. You've got to be able to bounce back all the time because there inevitably are ups and down. We try through preparation to maintain consistency all the way through and the more consistent you are the less time you take to bounce back. And that's the most important thing; always bounce back.

In 1977 I won the British Open title but a year later such was my confidence that I decided to fight a weight category up at the 1978 British Open. I got to the final in good form and was to meet Gilbert of France. Ahead in the match I made a tactical error and was caught on the ground with a submission choke that was to change my whole outlook on ground fighting for the rest of my life.

I was crushed. Just devastated, and I remember sitting there and a dear friend called Brian Perryman (who's not with us anymore) came up to me and said 'you needed that'. Then he walked off! And I remember thinking 'what the hell did he mean by that, I don't need that!' Tell you what I needed right then was to tell him exactly what I thought of him!

And of course as I reflect back on that moment he was absolutely right – I did need it because it made me re-focus and look at where I went wrong and the fact that I wasn't quite there; that supreme confidence, and even arrogance, was not enough.

I've had really big ups and downs throughout my career but I've maintained a certain standard all the way through that. I feel proud about that. I medalled, Senior and Junior, at 12 European Championships, 5 World Championships, 2 Olympic Games and 25 British Championships. So, even though I got some things wrong and sometimes *really* wrong, to the degree where I was mortified after the Olympic Games losses, mostly I got it right. If I did get it wrong I bounced back; if you don't you're finished. The trick is to remember the throws are psychological as well as physical. Everything bruises. Especially your confidence. Sometimes that can make you do things that you regret.

With the commentary, I see all the Champions and the ones working their way up and they're determined, they want to win, but you see the ones that handle it well and the ones that are on that line. It's a fine line between being able to handle it right and walking off without shaking hands – and people remember that, they don't remember the fight actually, they remember the fact you walked off and turned your back. Actually, they also remember when you really take it well – then you can walk off and kick the chairs in private! But people remember that in a nice way. I'm glad to say the majority of people remember me taking it in the right way.

That doesn't mean it wasn't hard. When I lost at the 1980 Olympics I was crushed. A lot of people talk about winning the bronze, winning the silver or winning the gold medal, but I *lost* the gold medal on two different occasions at Olympic two Games. I was absolutely devastated but I remember my lessons. I remember sitting there being interviewed. Of course I was very sad but I took it on the chin and praised the guys that beat me, they were great men of course. But of course they were, they had to be after all, they beat me in the final! Right?

Here's something that no one ever really thinks of and is the nucleus of my of these haunting feelings; Silver medallists are the only people on a Judo podium who've just lost. Everybody else has won. The two bronze medallists have won their matches and the gold medallist has beaten you. And you're the only one who has lost to get up there. It's a hard pill to swallow.

I had days where all I could think of was the fact I'd lost the Gold, and not won the Silver. These losses have weighed on me for a long, long time in fact, they most likely will always be with me. Oh I know, I hear you saying it, 'most people would be happy to get two Olympic medals and to be World Champion,' and yes that's a good achievement. For me, though, it wasn't enough because I knew that it could have been different.

I didn't hang the medals up, for years. In fact, they were in an old bag stuffed in a box shoved under the bed. Niki finally dusted them off, framed them and put them up in our office. When she did, it took me a long time to even look at them. It took a long time to accept the truth; it is an achievement. A great achievement. Now on reflection I have a different perspective on it.

I'll most likely always feel that twinge of disappointment, but that's just it, it's disappointment now more than devastation. 'Double Olympic medallist' - not many people can say that really, so it is a great achievement, not what I wanted but I'm really glad and fortunate I had the opportunity to showcase what I have. That I was also World Champion, and I did it in the way that I did, against the Japanese, with everybody in the world there. It makes me special and I'm always out to be different in some way or another.

I won seven European titles, Junior & Senior, I won the world titles, and I lost the Olympics and a World final on a split decision that could've gone my way so it very nearly went perfectly. I look back on my career now with a little bit of sadness, anger and frustration I suppose, because I believe I could've put those right. Or at least had the control to have done it right. Now, looking at the different reasons why it didn't quite happen, there are a lot of things but one that stands out is: preparation. Mental preparation is one of the biggest because certain times throughout my career when I look at a couple of my losses my mental preparation definitely wasn't right going into some of these events. I think that when I look at some of the athletes now when they're struggling to find form, one of the first things I ask them is 'how are things at home?' because it can make a massive difference. It might be their weight, it might be problems with a partner, it might be problems at home or financial problems, it can be any number of things that affect you. If you've got things on your mind it can affect your training and your mental approach to the competition – it starts from the mind, that's where the desire, the hunger, the need to succeed first starts

That's why Seoul went so wrong for me. It wasn't just the problems of my marriage either, but the inevitable split in focus you get when you become a husband and father. I was prepared for the '76, '80 and '84 Games although looking back it there were small things that could have changed the course. When my life changed so did my mindset. When I look back now at '88 I can see my preparation wasn't the same and it showed. I was still there, roundabout, but not quite at the same level as before. And I paid the price for that.

There is also the physical challenges you have to consider in Judo as well. I'm not just talking about training and fighting, but making weight. As a cadet u58kgs was the first European title that I won, then at U20s it was under 71kgs, which was light middleweight. At first at u71kgs I held the weight quite easily but then moved half way between this weight category and the one above.

Actually my natural weight was sitting somewhere between 71 and 78kgs and coming up to the 1980 Olympics it was a really difficult decision as to which category to fight in. Now of course they have qualification points from the World circuit to give them world rankings in order to qualify their places at the Olympic Games.

The top 12 for ladies and 22 for men automatically get qualification for the Olympics. But back then you could qualify through your country – so, as long as I was the best in my country, and I was selected, then they could send me to the Olympic Games. I was half way between two weight categories, I was about 75kgs/76kgs and I thought 'I've got to start experimenting here in the higher weight category, I've got to start preparing for it'

In 1980 when I won the Olympic silver medal in 71kg light middleweight, I put one of the reasons for the silver, in my opinion, down to the amount of weight I had to lose.

All the way through the Olympic qualifying year, 1979-80, I fought every competition in the higher weight category, u78kg, so as not to have to make the weight, and this meant all of the Grand Prix and Grand slam equivalent tournaments at the higher weight category as well as the European Championships. I won them all. So in reality, I beat everybody who was on that 1980 Olympic u78kg rostrum in all of the run up competitions.

The problem was that our Olympic seeding would only be taken from our previous World Championship results in 1979 which I got 3rd place in at u71kgs. So I was seeded going into the Olympic Games but at the category below. This put me in a dilemma. Do I drop the weight so that I am seeded or fight in the higher weight and go in as a wild card?

The seeding aspect is the key point because it can cost you the Olympic medal, if you haven't got a seeding you can get drawn against the number 2 or 3 in the world or even the number 1 in the world and if you're not on top form right away and you don't beat them you can lose your Olympic medal at the first hurdle. Whereas, if you are seeded there is a better chance of only meeting the very top fighters around the quarters or semi-finals. It makes a difference.

So I had to make the decision whether I was going to diet down and go in my seeded place where I would be seeded number 1 in the world going into my lower weight category or take my chances at the higher weight. I'd beaten everybody in the higher category that year so I had a choice of 2 great categories. I decided on the lower one as I could mostly control all those variables, such as the draw and weight, but I really struggled to make it. My weight then had drifted up to 76kgs and I was nearly at the top of the higher weight category. I dropped five or six kilos and did not lose the weight well.

Weight cuts are miserable and, when done badly, very dangerous. Look at contemporary MMA and you'll see the amount of high end fights that have been cancelled because someone was made sick by their weight cut and had to be rushed to hospital. There have even been some cases of death due to weight-cutting practices. Nowadays your diet is controlled down to the gram; protein, carbs and sugars all carefully balanced. The amount of expertise and availability of nutritional help is much better now giving fighters a much better chance of dieting safely. The problem with all weight loss for weight category sports is that you dehydrate down too, squeezing the water out of your body to make weight and then you immediately bulk back up once you've made weight. However, this doesn't always give you your strength back especially in time for when you need it most, like an Olympic final!

Now we are getting better at weight loss, making sure that the right nutritional help is given to the athletes. When I look back at my approach, I didn't do it well at all and in the end, in my Olympic final, I felt like I had no energy reserves to call upon.

Sports science in sport is imperative, and we need to train scientifically but we don't need to be ruled by sports science. At the end of the day as Judoka we need to go out there and fight. So you can think about the Rocky situation where you've got the Russian preparing with all of the modern training aids and sports science help. And then you've got Rocky fighting from the heart, with his basic, but fundamental, preparation – so we have to cater for that too, it's not all about sports science, but I really believe sports science plays an integral part of our preparation. I really believe that good dietary advice at that time would have probably meant my final would have been a more solid performance at any rate, but in reality drifted away from me in the end. I felt tired and lethargic and finally I lost on a split decision. So would it have made a difference? Yes most definitely. It would have made a difference in the latter part of the contest, it might have got me the decision. I believe that having to lose that amount of weight the way I did it made all the difference. But I'm not a 'would've and could've' kind of guy. It didn't happen. I did not do it right and I lost. Everyone on the rostrum I'd beaten at the European Championships, so bit disappointing. To say the least. Disappointing isn't the right word for it really. It's a mistake but a hell of a time in your life to make a mistake like that. It's life changing.

When I look back now at my career I think I got lots of things right. I tried to be consistent with my training and with my mental approach. In fact, I got more right than I did wrong. My record shows that; 12 European Championships medals; 5 World Championship medals and 2 Olympic silvers show my consistency. So there weren't many I didn't get almost right and the odd time of course I hit it spot on. That's what we're trying to do as coaches, get it as consistently right as we can. One of my mantras is 'consistency and persistency,' they are two of the most important elements.

I was at the top for over a decade and that's difficult in any sport. It is a very special gift if you've got the mental application to stick it, to carry on training day in and day out year in and year out. I say 'gift' as if you are born with it and a lot of people are and surely take it for granted, that everyone must have this as well. That's not the case, but nor is just being born with it. I think the gift is when you are able to recognise it, recognise the skill you have and use it, exploit it to the nth degree. Whether you need professionals to get or talk you there or you are able to do it yourself, it is something we all have. What differentiates us is the ability to understand how to use it effectively.

People still come to me now and ask for the secret. The only secret is you. If you have the heart for it there isn't a fight you can't win. If you don't want to do it or you've got doubts then it probably won't happen. If you really believe it and are willing to step across that line and be a pioneer then it can happen. It is hard being a pioneer and achieving something that nobody's done before but when you do it that's when people remember you. If you are a glory junkie, then that is the mother load right there! That is why people remember me beating the Japanese in the World Championships, because that middleweight category had never been won by anybody outside Japan and to do that against the Japanese in the final of the World Championships was something I believed I could do. I really believed it; if I hadn't, it wouldn't have happened.

That persistence and belief is something I truly believe is at the heart of Judo's global reach. The rest of the world are getting better with each passing year and we have athletes from outside of the motherland of Japan that are winning World and Olympic titles. However, when it comes to depth and the most world titles won, it's still the Japanese who lead the way. They have the system, they have 2.5 million people practicing Judo and they have the history. They'll tell you it's not the same as it was 20 or 30 years ago for them when they had 3 to 4 million people doing Judo but they still have a system that creates Judoka due to their incredible skills base. It comes back to the skills and the way to accumulate and develop them.

And, most importantly, learning how to lose. *Use that to make sure that next time, you win.*

Top: Chris with Neil
Bottom: Chris in wrestling outfit

17. Gentleman Chris Adams

I promised you I would talk about Chris and what tragically happened to him. It is a tough subject for me but also something I felt I needed to really delve into and come to terms with.

Chris and I were brought up with Judo as part of our everyday life. It started in Rugby, then on to Coventry and Solihull when we lived in Warwick.

We lived for our sport and almost every day was dedicated to improving our skills and our physical preparation.

Both of us wanted to excel and to perform and both of us had a drive and determination to be the best.

One of our best moments as kids growing up was when we were both winners at the Junior Nationals on the same day. We were both there in each other's corners supporting each other and of course celebrating our victories afterwards.

Chris was in the Senior National squad for many years and we were in the same team representing Great Britain in the Paris Tournament in 1978. It was one of the only times that we were to represent our Country together. To say that Chris was a handful was an understatement. He was hard to handle on the mat, difficult to throw and he was even harder to handle off the mat. He was strong willed and didn't like to play second fiddle to anyone.

He saw how much success his younger brother was having and I think that he knew deep down that it was going to be a tall order for him to get to the highest level in Judo. He was always looking for something more, a different direction. A chance for him to shine. Something that he could be the best at, he was desperate to make his own mark on life.

Someone suggested that he should try professional wrestling as he was a natural showman and he had great athletic ability. Of course he took to it like a duck to water and there he was on British television with the likes of Big Daddy, Mick McManus, Banger Walsh and Giant Haystacks.

He very quickly became the one to watch and soon became 'Gentleman Chris Adams' the English wrestler with flair and panache. He was a natural show-man.

It didn't take long before he was more famous than his brother who was lucky if he got 10 minutes on television once every four years. We often laughed about it and he often joked,

"What's it like being Chris Adams' brother?"

We joked, but he was always there for me and was very proud of my Judo achievements and supported me until the very end.

It didn't take long before he was spotted for the American Wrestling circuit and the WWF and I can still remember the big decision for him to up roots and move to America. It was an amazing opportunity for him to get onto the big stage, which was often up to 80,000 spectators in Madison Square Garden. What a journey from little old Leamington Spa Leisure Centre to one of the biggest stages on earth.

He was an instant success.

He also started his own wrestling school and was the first to introduce former American footballer Steve Williams, who would later be known as Stone Cold Steve Austin, to the wrestling game becoming his first mentor and advisor.

His drive and determination to do well in some ways was his undoing though. He went 100% at everything and with the wrestling business, that's a good thing but can be a very bad one. Drugs and alcohol played a big part in the wrestling fraternity mainly, I think, because of the incredible pressures put onto the performers and the gypsy lifestyle that they are forced to live.

The schedule those guys work is brutal. They drive themselves from venue to venue, have to pay for accommodation and food and petrol out of their own pocket and even at the highest level work hundreds of days of the year. The workload and pressure on them is immense, it really is, and the bangs and the scrapes they get are incredible. So many of them look for different ways to alleviate the pains and the stresses of the job and that means drugs and alcohol.

He was big into alcohol and he had real problems with his alcohol intake, to a degree where he had a mate of his who'd come round with crates full of brandy and that was just breakfast. No coffee, just alcohol.

Then tablets, the uppers and downers, it was madness, he was on a road to destruction and the alcohol and drugs were helping help him get there.

In 2001 I lead a seminar in Houston. It was post 9/11, only a few weeks after it happened, so Niki and I were undecided as to what to do. We were in a bit of a rough patch, living at the club, up in the office and had just received a succession of cancellations of courses to the amount of £4000, which to us at that time was everything, as we weren't making any money from the club. So I had to do it. That, along with the sentiment that we couldn't let people dictate our lives like that. Terrorists are just that and the only way to help stop it is not give in to the terror they spread. As well, I was looking forward to it because Chris had phoned the week before saying he would could down to Houston from Dallas where he was living to come see me. He had recently remarried and I hadn't seen him in a few years so a good catch up was in order.

He never made it.

The truth may never been told. I may never know exactly what went on and I can only go on the stories told to me by family and the police.

What seems to have transpired is Chris had received a call from his mate, Brent Parnall, the one that he got drunk with all the time and was his best man at his wedding to Karen. Parnall, high on drugs and alcohol phoned and told Chris he was going to commit suicide. Chris went over, en route, to check in on him on his way to see me in Houston.

He apparently tried to wrestle the gun off this Parnall and the gun went off. The bullet went straight through Chris' heart and that was it. He never made it down to see me. My brother was dead. My big brother, larger-than-life, pain-in-the-ass, wonderful man was gone from us. I just didn't know it yet.

Before he had set out to check in on Parnell, he gave Niki a call back in the UK to get the contact information for where I was and for some reason called my aunt Audrey, our favourite aunt just to have a chat. He did that sometimes, just usually in the wee hours of the morning.

Niki woke up at 1:30am that night, and sat bolt upright. She says she knew something was terribly wrong and had this over whelming sense to get a hold of me, to make sure I was alright. She felt that something had happened to me, something terrible. Such is the connection I had with my brother and then with Niki, I suspect.

She called everywhere with any number she had and finally had to give up as I was out for dinner with the hosts of the course, somewhat brooding as Chris hadn't showed up.

Niki tried to shake the ominous feeling and went back to sleep as she was taking Ashley to his rugby game in the morning.

She received a call from my mum while standing on the rugby sidelines. In fact it took her a few moments to realise it was my mum, as the person on the end of the phone was hysterical,

"He's dead, he's dead, he's dead, they found him, he's been shot! He's dead!'

'Jean? Woah, woah, woah, woah, who? Who's been shot, who's dead? Jean, tell me. Who?!'

'Chris, our Chris, Chris is dead he's been shot', Jean whispered.

It's one of those surreal moments, Niki said. She thought, 'Am I in a movie?'

My mum explained that the police in Dallas had called, there had been an altercation with a gun and Chris had been shot through the heart.

'Niki! He's dead, he's dead, he's gone.'

'Alright, Jean, listen to me. I need you to put the phone down, just stay calm, and let me wrap my head around this. Neil's over there, Jean, so I'll get word to Neil and he can take care of it from that end. Don't you worry, stay put, don't go out, don't call anybody, just stay put.'

She stood there looking at the game in play, her only thoughts were, 'I've got to tell Neil.'

It was 6 in the morning where I was, and nobody was awake, that was until the phone rang. There was a knock at my door with my host saying that Niki was on the phone and that it was urgent.

I came to the phone, 'what, what, Nik, its 6am', trying to sleep...'

That's when she told me.

'Neil,' she said through obvious tears, 'I'm so sorry. It's your brother, he's, your brother's gone...'

'What do you mean gone?' I was in shock.

'He's been shot, shot and killed, he's gone. He was trying to get to you but he got a call... Neil, you gotta say something, you still there?'

I don't think I even cried then, just complete shock. I even went on to do the session, as I had one more left to teach. I went into robot mode and got dressed and went and did the session.

It was pretty sombre as everyone on the mat was shocked at the news and probably more shocked that I was on the mat teaching, but I think I just went into auto pilot. Niki said she was going to take care of it, and I believed her. I guess I needed to as I was in a world of my own.

Niki had collected Mum and Dad and booked the plane tickets to get them out to Dallas the next day. It was like guiding two zombies around, they were just completely shell shocked.

My host drove me to Dallas to meet them at the airport and during the ride he looked at his mobile phone and saw he had a message from the evening before. He went deathly white and turned to look at me. Niki had given Chris his number as a point of contact and the message was from him. He handed the phone to me and I played the message.

'Hey Neil! Just on my way to see you. Really looking forward to it, Mate. Just got a call from a friend who seems to be in a little trouble, so going to stop in to see if he's alright on the way, and then I'm on my way to see you. Get ready, Neil!'

The first time Niki ever met Chris, was with him laid out. I remember turning to Niki and said, 'Chris, this is Niki,

Niki, this is Chris... but he doesn't look like Chris, it doesn't look like him'. Such was his sense of humour. I think we were all waiting for him to jump up and cry 'Gotcha!'

So I think it wasn't for real, I don't think it became really real to me until I couldn't call and talk to him.

So I arrived in America, taught Judo, and buried my brother.

I wish I could have helped, I think he was coming out of it himself and was realising that he needed another direction in his life. He realised he just couldn't do it anymore, and he was going to stop, but he was in the wrong place. It was to cost him his life.

He died because of alcohol and drugs really, because of him and his so called friend acting through induced stupidity. Of course it could have been murder because it was only the two of them. No one else was there. We only had his word about what happened that night. Parnall could have got the electric chair as it happens, but they believed him and he got off.

Never in your worst nightmares do you picture anything like that.

The strange thing about the whole thing was that it was like an episode of *Dallas* or some soap opera. Ironic is the fact that he was coming from Dallas. It was one of those things in TV programmes, he wrestled the gun and the gun went off and it happened, it happened like that. It was a tragedy and he was only 46 years of age.

I think what really saddens me most is his wonderful family he has left behind. His wonderful son Chris who has grown into an amazing man, his beautiful daughters Jade and Julia: all of these are a spitting image of Chris's good looks, and his four incredible grandchildren. He will never see them grow up but I will never stop telling them what an amazing man he was.

He always had an addictive personality. In fact, when I

think of it, we both had.

I guess I drew my strength to stop from all of these things that had gone wrong with Chris, as well as myself. It made Niki and I more determined to make everything work and that's why I know I'm so determined that it will never ruin my life again or affect my family. I'll never have another drink, I know that for a fact.

It is not just you it affects when you go this way it's the people around you and often the people closest to you.

I wish that I had lived closer to Chris and could have helped him. It doesn't matter what help you get though in the end, as I said in the beginning, it has to come from you. You have to want to do it. I just wish that I didn't have to lose my brother in the process.

The Adams Family: Neil, Niki, Ashley, Brooke and Taylor

18. How I Live Now

My life sits between two extremes. On the one hand there's near constant travel. As I write this I just got back from one trip and have two more back to back ones coming up. It's pretty nonstop and I think my record is 8 countries in 10 days including connections. It's crazy sometimes and it can grind you down. Trust me, there are few sensations odder than being in Moscow Airport and suddenly realising you have no idea where you are!

And on the flip side of that, I'm a husband and a dad. Professional athletes get looked after a great deal, like I've talked about, but we also fend for ourselves a lot. I was very lucky because my mum made sure I was able to look after myself from an early age. In fact, you know what one of the first things I ever learned to do was? Sew up my trousers because they were always splitting. She taught me to pick a stitch. Plus, I learned how to iron early because mum hated it. She taught me so she wouldn't have to, I'm sure!

I cook too, iron my own stuff, and get my gear ready. It's necessary and it helps because between the job, the travel, getting the girls ready for school and their activities, and having a life there's not much spare time.

It gets a bit too much sometimes. I did at least 28 countries last year and a big part of that lands at the end of the year. The Asian tour does Japan, Korea, China, Kazakhstan, and Uzbekistan, then in the middle of that they put in Abu Dhabi as well and by the time I get back for Christmas I've just about had enough.

I love being at home.
Except for the ironing.
Especially as Nik's not as good at as me.
She hates ironing.

Of all the places I've been, I think New Zealand is my favourite. I did two weeks in New Zealand and we travelled round the north and south islands. It was like a mini Canada in that you've got the mountains, you've got the Plains, Wine Country, thick forest, and flat hot springs, the climate is hot to not, and the geography changes constantly. We had a boat ride in one of the gorges, and we went swimming with the dolphins.

It was excellent, I loved it, even though I was ill when I was there. I had a temperature of 103 and I had to deliver seminars all over the country, which wasn't very good, but the country was just breathtaking. This one morning everybody was going out to swim with the dolphins and with this fever, I obviously couldn't go. I was watching them all put their wet suits on when suddenly I jumped up and said 'I'm going! That's it, I'm going!' I don't know whether it was the illness or what but as I slid into the water these dolphins were swimming round me and between my legs, I don't know whether they sensed I wasn't well but they were around me. It was very reassuring and somehow I knew they knew I might need help - I was the first one in and the last one out of the water. It was the most amazing experience!

They took us to look at The Bridge To Nowhere, up in the hills, deep in this gorge, where they put a lot of the people who came back from the First World War and they gave them land to farm. There was a bridge, they call it 'the bridge to nowhere' and it is just that! All of a sudden, in the thick, thick forest, there is this cement bridge spanning the gorge. There is no road leading to it and there is no road leading from it. You went over the bridge and that's it; it stops! Of course, all the vegetation and land had been reclaimed, where the people had houses and the farmers had farmed. Mother Nature had it back and when you did stop to look and take in deeper the surrounding flora and fauna, you could make out the forms of old chimney breasts, half walls, and home hearths - it was quite amazing. We've said that one day we'll do a kayak trip or a canoe ride all the way down the river, I wouldn't mind doing that over a 3 day trip.

I had organised it so I could take a select team of the Welsh players along with us and use the trip as a training camp and it also served as a team building exercise, none more than the bungee jumping which all the kids were keen to do. To say I'm not great with heights is an understatement, so I elected to watch them all from the viewing tower on the side of the gorge.

Niki and I were their own cheerleading squad on the side line every time one of them nose dived off the bridge platform. That was until the youngest of the team with us, Sara Connelly walked out onto the platform. She looked over the edge and turned around to face the guide. We were a bit disappointed for her as it looked like she bottled it. As she was the last one to jump, we started to turn around to go back to the reception area, when someone shouted, 'She's going for it!' And there she went. Not only did she jump, but she did a most graceful swan dive out into the open air. Cheers could be heard from the bridge and of course we were going wild on the ground, so happy she had faced it and went for it.

When she returned to us, there were high fives all around and I asked her, 'Sara, what did he say up there to change your mind?' curious to know what tactic he had employed.

'He told me I wouldn't get my money back.'

And then there's Canada. Niki gets desperate to go back home and her limit seems to be 2 years maximum. I get it. She gets home sick and just needs to top up for a while. We often arrange seminars in Canada so that we can visit family and friends. Normally it is for a few weeks at a time and will mean travelling from Toronto to Montreal and then over to Manitoba where Niki grew up. Typical of what you would think of a Prairie landscape is Niki's family's farm. It spans the 'quarter section', which I found out translates to a ½ mile by ½ mile of the patchwork quilt design of the Canadian Prairies. Her mum and dad built a large log house on the farm along with a blacksmith's shop and an old hayshed that doubles as a teaching area for blacksmithing workshops and craft lessons that the family host there. I can see why Niki needs to come back from time to time as it is a healing place, a real sanctuary where time seems to stop, just enough to catch your breath and try something different as there is always something to do or experience. The girls love it there.

Meeting her parents for the first time was to set the tone for what would be a wonderful understanding of how future life would be with Niki. Pam is the hostess with the mostest and makes sure you eat your weight with one of her famous breakfasts before heading out anywhere. And her Dad, Tom, who we have sadly lost, ensured I knew who was number one with his daughter.

I was sitting in the living area, in a big comfy chair just taking in the hand-made items that the family had made over the years, trying to get a sense of what Niki's childhood might have been like and knowing how much this place meant to her, trying to be a part of it myself. Tom walked into the room to momentarily break my thoughts, which immediately, went to Oh no! I'm in his chair! Up I sprung out of the chair, exclaiming, 'Sorry Tom! Is this your chair?'

Without a pause, but just a blink, Tom stated, 'They're all my fucking chairs.' And walked to his chair across from me. Then the smirk came, 'Ah sit down you Brit. Relax. You guys are all so uptight.'

And that was… *is* the way of it with Niki and her family. The lovely, comfortable banter that makes one feel wanted, and a part of a family. Not that I'm not extremely happy that there are now other spouses that have joined in to take some of the heat off. Whew! Thankful for small mercies.

I remember cutting the grass for Pam, on the riding lawn mower, and there is this one stretch of lawn sandwiched in between 2 sets of pine trees. Well, thanks to me, it is now dubbed 'Mosquito Alley' as when I finally was able to flee the area, I sprinted to the house with this buzzing that sounded like a squadron of airplanes following me. I slammed the door, and was sure the next time I would open it I would see the horde of little bastards stuck in the door like thumbtacks on a cork board. The door-slam shook the house and brought the family clamouring into the hall.

'What the hell, Neil?' Niki questioned through a furrowed brow from within the amassed Jenkins family in the hall.
'Mosquitos,' I replied. 'I think I just discovered Mosquito Alley!'
'Ahhh,' they all responded in unison, nodding their heads matter of factly, and as it was a part of their everyday life turned and left the room to carrying on with whatever I had interrupted and left me searching for Calamine lotion.

A lot of people say: 'it must be great visiting all these countries, what a life!' and it used to be tremendously exciting. Now, though, it's tiring. This is a hard life, doing this as a journalist more than a competitor. It can be too much. Which is why we make sure that we do so much as a family that is separate from our working schedule.

I love being out in nature. Niki and I go for walks whenever we can. There are some amazing paths and walks around our house and we sneak off whenever we can. That's the beauty of working for yourself. You can always ask the boss for the afternoon off.

But the first place I go after a long trip is the garden. I'll either cut the lawn or do a bit of weeding; and the reason for that is that it grounds me. No matter where I've been, what country I've been to or what I've done, people I've met; this is my life this is where I would rather be. It's about cutting the lawn, cutting the edges, making sure the weeds are up. For me it's a really good grounding experience. When I've done that, I find I can relax.

If we are really stressed we go in the hot tub. Not a traditional English activity but one that has been adopted through my Canadian connections. It was a little odd at first, (Being outside! In a bath?!) but Niki insisted. She wanted it to help with my hip rehabilitation, which I have to say was a miracle to have.

In fact, let's talk about the Canada thing for a minute. Because of the accent, a lot of people mistake Niki for an American and of course she's not. In fact, culturally they are different but it is amazing how many folk do not know the difference. Canada is definitely closer to our culture than America, especially in Vancouver.

They call Manitoba the Land of the Big Sky. There is nothing to break the horizon, when the sun comes up you can see it go right across the sky until it lands. In the summer they have long days. It's the most beautiful country. Just prior to getting married Niki and I visited Fort McMurray, Alberta in the North of Canada. We then travelled right down through the Rocky Mountains by train right through to Vancouver. From there we went by plane to Toronto where we got married. Now of course after 14 wonderful years married and 16 years together we have our two beautiful girls and an interesting family life. From a cultural point of view it's wonderful. We have mixed cultures in the house which is nice. Sometimes our cultures cross over but the way we both think is pretty much the same which is marvellous really. Tomaytoes and Tomartoes is one of them but the first, 'Kulaala Lumpuuuur' still sticks with me.

Bob, Aidan, Wicca, Gypsy and Tilly (and Neil)

19. Two Legs + Four Legs = Family

I remember the very first time I saw Bob.

It was Christmas 1985 and this cute, little puppy was staring at me from the top of the stairs. It was a beautiful blond Labrador and it's funny how he was everybody's dog that Christmas, that is until he started to do his business on the floor, then, suddenly, he was all mine.

I didn't know then that he was going to become my best friend and constant companion for 15 years. He was super intelligent and very amusing, but as with all dogs he could be tiring with his constant need for attention. I only needed to twitch and he was by my side ready for a walk.

He was the best dog that anybody could wish to have. Everybody loved him, and he was everybody's friend. He didn't have a bad bone in his body and I remember Ashley climbing all over him when he was a baby and Bob wouldn't bat an eyelid. He was so kind, giving, and protective too.

When we moved to France and Ashley was just one year old, everybody, including Bob came too. I remember Bob being just as miserable as everybody else. Everyone was happy to be coming home but the worst thing was that when we returned to England, I had to put him in quarantine for six months.

I remember his face when I put him in a box and had to say goodbye. He somehow knew I was leaving him. I was told that it would be better not to visit him at the kennels as he would just think that I was leaving him every single time. It would frazzle him too much and make him anxious and pine for us. Better to be just the once. My heart broke that day leaving him there and it took everything in my being not to go and visit him, if only to let him know I hadn't abandoned him. That was a long six months. I remember the day going to collect him after the long sojourn away, and he saw me through the fence. He went berserk to try to get to me. He had put on weight because he normally ran with me on a daily basis and was in good condition when I'd left him. Six months in the kennel had not been good to him.

He went into the back of the car like a missile. Happy to be going home, but then was so angry with me that it took me quite a few weeks to get my relationship with him back on track.

I had felt so guilty about leaving him, but at the time that was the system and we couldn't do anything about it.

We had some amazing times with Bob and he did some amazing things. He could count, he never left my side if I didn't want him to, and he could carry the largest, longest sticks on earth and navigate them through the narrowest of spaces without dropping it. One time I offered him a treat and told him to sit. I put the treat on top of the chair ready for him to take it on my command. The telephone then went and I answered the call, forgetting about poor Bob. When I returned 10 minutes later, there was a puddle of saliva and a very controlled Labrador still waiting for my command.

As he became older he became everybody's dog again and I remember looking at him when it suddenly hit me that he had such bad arthritis and that he was an old man now. Gentle walks took the place of the runs and we limited the amount of stick throwing and ball fetching.

I remember Philip, Alison's stepfather who trained gun-dogs, saying to me at the time that it might be time for Bob to be put down as he was having problems to walk properly in the end. I was annoyed at the suggestion and probably made it known I was so. However, he was absolutely right when I look back. I did keep Bob for maybe a year too long but I found it so difficult to say goodbye to my old friend.

In the end, the decision was made for me when I came down one day and Bob couldn't move. He was lying in his own mess. I phoned the vet who came and we said our last goodbyes to the most wonderful friend anyone could wish to have.

I had a job to get through the task of burying him. He's at the house in Canley in the garden under the big tree. It was hard to leave him there as well, when I left the house, however nothing to be done about that.

After I buried Bob I said that that was it! I wouldn't have another animal ever again. They are with you such a short period of time and absolutely take over your emotions. It is the unconditional love that they give. I guess that was so attractive to me as well, as they don't judge. He was so very helpful through the years where I felt like everyone was judging me and not really understanding what I was going through. None of that with Bob, just love, understanding and at times, someone to talk to! I could count on him to be there and be supportive no matter what.

Niki and I had often talked about getting another animal but because I was travelling so much it would've been her responsibility to look after it.

If it was a dog it would have restricted our movements in our free time and so we decided that it would wait until the right moment came up.

She did mention the possibility of getting a cat and I have to say that never having had a cat before, I wasn't too keen on the idea. I always felt that their independence and lack of total dependency on me would in no way be able to compete with my relationship with Bob. With cats, I believed, it is an absolute, conditional love and completely on their terms. How wrong I was. They are totally different to dogs, but I am in awe and respect of their independence and their individuality. I love that about them!

Our first cat, Aidan, came to us by accident. We were living in Belgium and I was teaching at the National Centre in Zele. We were ready to carry on for a day trip to Bruges, one of our favourite places to visit and one of the girls spotted this little black ball of fur underneath a car in the car park. Needless to say this little ball of fur came with us to Bruges, securely stowed in Niki's handbag. He toured Bruges with us and was a complete distraction from the wonderful architecture featuring in many a Japanese tourists' pictures, sitting quietly and hanging out of Niki's purse. I protested it all the way there, all around the town and all the way home. And I was completely ignored by the females of the family, meaning the whole family but me. Niki suggested we make FOUND! Posters to send to the Judo club on the Monday, but as it was Saturday night, the office wasn't open, nor was it on Sunday, so the kitten would have to stay with us for the weekend. When Niki announced the time to make the posters, I looked up from my chair and a purring kitten on my lap and said,

'What posters?'

The posters never got made and Aidan quickly became a member of the family. He was a super cat with a great personality and had a tendency to climb on your shoulder and perch there like a parrot.

Niki's father, Tom had always said and taught her that pets should be in pairs. A friend of Niki's one day asked her come to her farm to look at some kittens that her cat had just had and Niki returned with our second cat, Wicca. We had a certain amount of time where Aidan had to show her who was boss as he was the man of the house, and poor Wicca had to put up with him... for a time. She bided her time and in a blink, Aidan knew his place! They became close friends though and in the end they relied on and loved each other.

Both of our Belgian cats came with us back to England and settled in nicely in our Rugby house and had lots of fields and garden to roam in each day. Thank goodness the quarantine laws had been relaxed by then and we wouldn't have to wait 6 months for them when we left.

They had a wonderful life but were taken from us too early. Poor Aidan had a problem with his nose and was having problems breathing properly. This resulted in him losing weight and he was also having problems with his pads on his paws. He found it difficult to walk properly in the end so we took him to the vets who put him under anaesthetic to do a small operation on his nose. Later that week we had a call from the vet asking us to bring him in for more tests. Poor Aidan never came out of the anaesthetic, and we understand that he had a heart attack on the table. I remember Niki phoning me in a flood of tears. I broke down immediately myself. We were both devastated with his loss. I don't think either of us realised just how close and how much he meant to us.

Then poor Wicca was looking for Aidan for the whole of the next week, and it was because of this that she ventured out onto the main road near our house. Just two weeks after Aidan died, we lost Wicca too. Another phone call from Niki broke the news to me when I was abroad working and again we were both devastated. It is incredible how animals can climb into your hearts and become part of your family. Once again I said never again will I get close to an animal, or should I say let an animal get close to me.

That soon changed. I missed the undercurrent of energy the cats gave to the house. I missed how they met me at the door for a pet and then buggered off as if to say, 'ok you've had enough'.

In September 2015, Niki and I decided to look at the possibility of getting a kitten as the girls were desperate for a pet again, and the pressure was on to have a look. We looked at a beautiful black kitten with eyes like big, yellow saucers. Of course we came back with her. The girls and both Niki and I fell for her straight away. So here we were again in a situation where an animal was in our hearts. Once again though we thought it would be better if there were two of them together, to keep each other company. Just a couple of weeks after getting Gypsy our black cat, we brought Tilly home, a tortoiseshell. They were two bundles of fur together and being that they were so young, they thought of each other as sisters from the very beginning.

They are so much a part of the family that it's hard to think of a time without them. I have been so lucky to have some amazing pets and they're lucky to be part of such a wonderful family.

***

My home life is blessed, there is no other word I can think of. Especially since 2012 when we came back to Rugby. That was great. Strange, but lovely. We had owned this house since 2003 but not ever lived in it renovated until now. It was like moving into a new house wrapped in the familiarity of the area. Here we were, living in the house that we originally bought to do up as a project and here we were again, making it our home. It was really nice being part of the village community and I know that Niki really enjoys having so many friends close by.

Being back in the UK, I think it makes me realise just how British I am and how much I've missed not only the culture, but my family. The love that we have as a family is the most important thing to have and it is the most important ingredient. My brother always used to say to me that it's family first and he was right. Niki and I have known each other 16 years and have been through some really difficult times, as you have read, but we have grown together closer and stronger and have an incredible bond that I believe, and hope, all people should experience.

She's not only my best friend but she is my rock. She is the kindest, funniest, and fiercely protective person that I have ever met and our life together from the second we wake up until we go to sleep is full of laughter, love, passion, and happiness.

From a financial point of view it has not been easy for us and even now we seem to be pushing hard in order to create my legacy and to pass on my experience and my skill sets to others. I don't know if we'll ever be millionaires but when it comes to love we both hit the jackpot.

Sometimes I hear people discussing what is the perfect age to be? If they could go back in time what would be the best time for them. I think looking back from a physical point of view and having many of my first experiences behind me, I would say that 35 would be a good age to be. Most of the physical parts still work and I think that many of our past experiences give us a different perspective on life. Saying this and on reflection I had some pretty big lessons to learn from 35 years on. I love where my life is now and the direction that it is heading, it is the happiest I've felt in my life emotionally, although I wouldn't mind having my 35 year old body back.

I have a beautiful family. I have my rock, my best friend and the Love of my Life in Niki and if it's possible our love just grows stronger by the day. Somebody wanted us to meet and all those stars were aligned to bring us together in Sydney. It was the best thing to ever happen to me. Maybe I was looking to the wrong stars to align all those years ago or maybe wishing on the wrong thing.

Ashley is now approaching 30 and has grown into a great man and person and has a magical relationship with his sisters, Brooke and Taylor, my two beautiful daughters who have their dad well and truly wrapped around their little fingers.

Our house is full of laughter and happiness and the future looks good. We must ensure that we stay true to ourselves, keep asking the hard questions and not dodging the answers.

Neil

20. Bowing Off

I got asked a question not long ago about what super power I'd like to have and I think that what I'd like is foresight. I think that, when you're younger this is what you haven't got, you haven't got the experience to see things before they happen. We hear it so often, 'I wish I knew then what I know now', and I think to have that foresight and that experience to have made better decisions when I was younger, that would have been really advantageous to me. I would have amended the drink situation at an earlier stage and that would really have been of benefit to me. To have taken certain steps from an educational point of view would have helped my career and probably given me a better idea on direction for life after competition. There are many things from a relationship point of view that could have been done differently.

But foresight is an exceptional thing, something all of us

at one point would have liked to have enjoyed. However, it's something we learn from experience, and without those experiences we wouldn't be us, and we would be rather boring, I assume. Niki has always said to me that she has no regrets, only bad experiences, and I think she's right. It's all lessons to be learned and form us as individuals. It's just the control freak in me wants to be prepared and it always seems when I'm not completely prepared, or take that all-important beat to think things through, that is when things go pear shaped. And not just a little it seems, but mega. Having foresight would be less exhausting I must admit.

When I was 23 years old, Nicholas Soames asked me if I'd like to do a biography. At the time I agreed and Nicholas did a good job but it bothered me calling it a biography. Calling it a biography is ok but of course at 23 years of age it is not a life story. It is a story so far. It wasn't a complete story. I was still competing. I was 23 years old with my whole life ahead of me. We should have called it something different, like: 'My story so far' or 'My Life: Chapter 1'.

This story is my second chapter. It is the last 30 years and I have to say that it has been a bit of a roller coaster. 'A Second Life in Judo'. The last 30 years were more eventful than the first 23, even though competition-wise I achieved a lot. So it's two different lives really with some real ups and downs.

I feel the last 30 years are more interesting which is why we want to do the second part of this now. The earlier one has early relationships, preparation, the way I felt going into competitions. I was glad to bring that book out but of course when we wrote the first one, the '*me*' that was coming out was different to the one that's sitting in front of you now because it was a different part of my life. I was at a different stage of my life. When I was narrating the first book I was a confident, arrogant person with a very positive directive. I like to think that I have always been a nice person but over the second part of my life I have learnt to be a quieter, more controlled person with humility and above all, experience. I like me better now.

I like to feel I was always a good person, but I was certainly selfish in my traits and ways and I feel that first book came out like that. Nicholas wrote it like I was saying it and quite rightly so, so when I was saying 'I didn't like the way it was written', I didn't like the way I came over in the book. Don't get me wrong. Nicholas was brilliant, it was me. I didn't come over as I wanted me to come over.

My last 16 years since Niki and I have been together, we've grown together but I've grown, personally in so many ways. Inside I'd like to think I am the same man you read about in the first book. I am still determined, I hate losing at anything I do – whether it's at tiddlywinks or whatever - but I accept it that sometimes it happens, there are things I can't do now that I could at 23.

Sometimes I find that difficult to accept but I'd like to think more than anything that I can express myself a lot better than I did then. I love the commentary and it's interesting looking at how I was and now how I've grown to be able to express myself on camera and changed my approach over the past 30 years.

That's what I'm talking about when saying about somebody writing a biography at 23 years of age. To call it a biography, or a *Life Story* is ridiculous, you can only call it information of a certain time in your life, or *Life as I Know It Now*

So what if I had the superpower chance to tell myself, way back then, everything that was going to happen.

Would I?

Absolutely.

I'd sit myself down and say 'get your direction sorted and you need to be slightly more thoughtful in some of your decisions you make'. I've definitely become more reflective on things and definitely toned down my attitude on how I treat people. I'd definitely change some things. That is the advice I'd give, I would take a while to think about what you do because actions can get you into trouble. I talked earlier about legacy and if there's one thing I've learned it's this; we are all in charge of our own legacy.

One last story and then I'll let you get on with your own lives, I promise.

Niki and I were once in a churchyard in St Just, Cornwall one family holiday. We enjoy visiting old churches and often check out the dates on the headstones as Niki, *ever* the Canadian, loves seeing just how old things are here. There was a big tombstone and it caught my eye, not only because of its size, for it was big, at least 4 feet tall, but because it had an unusual amount of writing on it. It didn't just give the birth date and the date of his passing, it gave the reader more. I'm sure anyone who is reading this and has been to St Just in Roseland will know what I'm talking about, and most likely can't help but smile.

It told you a little of this man's personality, it gave you a glimpse of what he had done with his life, and you suddenly felt an empathy towards the family as you, too, suddenly missed him, or the fact that you missed meeting him.

I think that is what we all should strive for. Not only to be known for what and/or who you are, but also for what you are all about. Be known for your legacy and make that legacy, not only about you, but about your relationship with others, so when the Bards sing your song, it makes people smile and feel that they too can have something to give.

FOXGLOVES

Image Contents

FOXGLOVES

foxglovesmartialarts.com
foxspirit.co.uk

Images copyright © David Finch
Reproduced with permission
Neil & Yamashita
'80 Olympic Medal shot out of Gi
Neil preparing on mat
Seoul fight fighting Portugal
Nevzerov
Neil running at Crystal Palace training
'96 Coaching Team sidelines
IJF Hall of Fame
'84 Podium pictures

Adams Family Photos images copyright © Neil Adams
Cyril coaching Chris & Neil
Neil in France with Bob & Ashley
The Old Club
House in Canley, Coventry
Neil & Niki
Furze Barns, Rugby
Chris Adams
Adams Family
Adams Family Pets
Neil

Copyright © Stanislaw Michalowski
Reproduced with permission.
Amelie R and Neil at u23 European final

FOXGLOVES

Neil Adams MBE is the World renowned 8th Dan Judoka who takes Martial Arts to a higher level.

He has won a plethora of medals and competitions, including World Championships in 1981 and two Olympic Silver medals in Moscow 1980, and Los Angeles in 1984. He has been Olympic Coach for Great Britain and Belgium, National Coach for Wales and is a member of the International Judo Federation (IJF) & European Judo Union (EJU) Expert Commissions.

He has now turned his expert hand to aiding those up and coming martial artists, providing technical advice and expertise on an individual basis.

Neil's goal is to provide an arena for every level of martial artist where they can gain technical knowledge and insight in an individual environment as well as on a competitive platform.

Neil Adams Effective Fighting Ltd is a family owned, family run business. With wife, former Canadian Judo Olympian Niki (Jenkins) and their 3 children, Ashley, Brooke & Taylor, they together are looking to raise the profile of Judo around the world and into every home.

You can find out more about Neil Adam's Effective Fighting at the website
http://www.neiladamsjudo.info/
or follow him on
twitter: @NeilAdamsJudo
&
Facebook: www.facebook.com/NeilAdamsJudo

Printed in Great Britain
by Amazon